AN UPSTART IN GOVERNMENT

'Arun Maira has a passion for the progress of India and improvement of the lives of its poorest people. This must be a collaborative endeavour, he urges, and suggests systematic ways to engender cooperation. He also provides insights from his decades of experience in making in India and abroad for changes in mindsets necessary to create millions more good jobs in manufacturing in India. An inspiring book.'

Suresh Prabhu,
Minister for Railways, Government of India

'In this very readable account drawn from several decades of practical experience, Arun Maira offers powerful perspectives on how we can shape our future. In highlighting the role that cooperation between stakeholders plays in institutional reform, his deep faith in people as "appreciating assets" comes through very strongly. This work is a timely and valuable contribution to thinking about the reform agenda that India must embrace.'

Cyrus P. Mistry,
Chairman, Tata Group

'Arun Maira has brought his vast experience, first in the private sector and then as a member of the Planning Commission to bear on this thoughtful book about building methods of cooperation and consensus to tackle some of the seemingly intractable challenges that face India. As he points out, the stalemate that bedevils decisions arising out of protagonists taking adversarial positions, can often be solved by getting everyone to cooperate using proven methods. This is an important book from someone who after a distinguished career in the private sector, has seen the Government from the inside.'

Nandan Nilekani,
Co-founder of Infosys, and former chairman of Aaadhar

'Arun Maira has a passion for helping people to listen to each other, and to work more effectively together to produce the results they would all want. He brought this passion, which was evident in his earlier work as a leader of manufacturing organizations and as a consultant, to his work in the Planning Commission. In his book, *An Upstart in Government*, he explains how India's Total Factor Productivity would increase and how much the people of India would benefit if systematic processes were applied for consultative planning and coordinated implementation. He explains the principles for creating cooperation systems with many examples. His book must be read by leaders in government, in the private sector, and in civil society organizations also. They must all create better cooperation systems within their enterprises. And, for the nation to progress much faster and bring the fruits of progress to all Indians, they must cooperate more effectively with each other too.'

Anand Mahindra,
Chairman, Mahindra and Mahindra

'The title of Arun Maira's book, *An Upstart in Government*, clarifies at the outset that he was a different kind of government functionary. His book manages to "talk of many things," like Alice's Walrus, with true anecdotes and stories of his experiences in various sectors, without bureaucratic and management jargons, and is very easy reading. To be able to see the larger picture, project a sensible worldview and yet be able to connect with the human interest concerns of the common man, as he does, is an urgent need of our time.

My own growing concern of the need for Anubandh, of concern and connectedness among people, communities and even countries finds an echo in his book, in which he explains how leaders in government, those in the private sector, as well as the people in civil society organizations must have greater cooperation with each other. For the nation to progress faster, and bring the fruits of progress to all Indians, they must cooperate more effectively with each other too. This is a book that will appeal to both those in the government and those not in it.'

Ela R. Bhatt,
Founder, SEWA

AN UPSTART IN GOVERNMENT

Journeys of Change and Learning

Arun Maira

RUPA

Published by
Rupa Publications India Pvt. Ltd 2015
7/16, Ansari Road, Daryaganj
New Delhi 110002

Sales Centres:

Allahabad Bengaluru Chennai
Hyderabad Jaipur Kathmandu
Kolkata Mumbai

ISBN: 978-81-291-3718-0

Second impression 2015

10 9 8 7 6 5 4 3 2

The moral right of the author has been asserted.

For my father and mother

Contents

Prologue: The Writer and the Journey   ix

Part One
An Upstart in Government

1. To Serve the Country   3
2. Tripping Through Red Tape   10
3. A Child's Ambition   20
4. A Road Less Taken   26
5. Playing the Inner Game: Make in India   32
6. Made by India: David Takes on Goliaths   41
7. No Time to Kill Time   46
8. An Innovative Enterprise   56
9. Crises of Aspiration   67

Part Two
Shaping Our Future

1. My Grandson's Advice   75
2. Change It if You Can   79
3. A Strategy for Change   85
4. Connecting the Dots   94
5. When the People Speak   101
6. Many Dancers, One Dance   115
7. Shaping the Future   122
8. The Change Begins   139
9. Discovering Our Way   147

Part Three
Learning to Work Together

1.	Collaborating and Coordinating	161
2.	The India Backbone Implementation Nework (IbIn)	169
3.	Making It Easier to 'Make in India'	176
4.	Building Bridges for Trust	190
5.	Delivering Change	205
6.	Rusting and Resisting Change	215
7.	Cooperation Systems	227

Epilogue: Ends and Beginnings	235
My Plan	238
Acknowledgements	243
Index	245

THE WRITER AND THE JOURNEY

A reader looks at the introduction of a book to know what it is about and how it is constructed. When an author begins to write, he also wonders what his book will be about and how he will write it.

Paul Theroux, who has written famous travel books such as *The Great Railway Bazaar,* reflected on these questions at the Jaipur Literature Festival in January 2015. In a panel with other travel writers, he was asked what the difference was between writing a novel, which he admitted is his passion, and writing travel books, which he excels at. The difference, he said, was that in a travel book you know what you are going to write about. In a novel, you discover what you are writing about as you write. Travel books, biographies, autobiographies, and histories record what has happened: they are 'non-fiction' literature. In a novel, you make up the facts to tell a story that is a 'fiction' of the author's imagination. The novelist creates facts, and does not know what facts he will create when he begins to write.

V.S. Naipaul, the Nobel Laureate in Literature, whom Theroux had greatly admired and with whom he had had a nasty public falling out, was also at the Jaipur Literature Festival. Naipaul has written many famous books—including several on India, a country that has fascinated him because his forefathers migrated from India to the Caribbean islands. One of his lesser-known books, *A Way in the World*[*] is a collection of his reflections, many autobiographical, strung together in a book he calls a novel. In one of its chapters, 'New Clothes: An Unwritten Story', Naipaul considers how he should write a story about a traveller in a part of South America he, the author, has visited. How the place and the people in it are described will depend on who the novelist chooses as the traveller and narrator, he says. Therefore, he wonders who the narrator of the story should be...

This book before the reader is not fiction and I will be the narrator of the stories in it of journeys of change and learning.

One is about the fulfilment of a young boy's aspiration, born within him soon after India became independent, to work in the government and serve his country. His aspiration is fulfilled fifty years later, when he thinks he has retired and found time at last to learn to play the leisurely game of golf after a long innings in the private sector. A telephone call out of the blue from the prime minister of India asking him to join the government to serve the country compels him to put his new golf set aside and get back to work.

Another story is about the future of India, a country in transition, and about the hopes and frustrations of its people who aspire for a better world for themselves, their children, and grandchildren. Through this story runs the theme of people learning to work together. India is one of the most beautifully diverse nations in the world. It is admired for its spirit of democracy. Discord amongst India's diverse and democratic citizens often seems to slow its progress. Its citizens must learn to cooperate to create a future that is good for all Indians.

A third story is an account of the reform of the Planning Commission of India, which this upstart in the government

---

*V.S. Naipaul. *A Way in the World*. Vintage, 1995.

became engaged with, and of efforts to introduce new ways of planning and getting things done. Reforming a hoary old institution set in its ways, from within, is never easy, even when many feel it must be reformed, as did the prime minister of India. Unorthodox ways had to be found to introduce innovations into the Commission and in the way planning was being done. The vision of what the Planning Commission should transform into that emerged from these innovations, has found a home in the charter of the new NITI (National Institution for Transforming India) Aayog, which was formed in January 2015 to replace the Planning Commission.

There is also a story of an unusual start-up within government which enabled these innovations to be made inside the old institution, and to thus begin the redesign of an old aeroplane while it was flying. Many inspiring stories have been written about entrepreneurs and start-ups who, working out of garages, outside the constraints of old institutions, have created new institutions around new ideas. There are fewer stories about 'intrapreneurs', even in the private sector, who burrow for change from within the boundaries of old institutions that are tied up by their rules and traditions. This story is about a small team of intrapreneurs within the government, where old ways are even more firmly tied up in red tape.

The stories weave through each other. As Naipaul said, who the narrator is and what he is describing cannot be entirely separated. In these stories the changers cannot be separated from what is being changed.

I have been a manager and a management consultant for forty-five years. Following this, I served for five intense years in India's Planning Commission until June 2014. When I was writing this book, my friends asked me, will it be a 'management' book or a 'policy' book? In which section of a bookshop, or under which category on Amazon should my book be placed? This is a 'crossover' book which would interest managers in business and managers in government. I hope that it will engage policymakers on both sides. I have realized that there is a lot we can learn from each other, and that we must work more effectively together to improve the world for everyone.

Part One

An Upstart in Government

◆

If you do not know where you want to go,
you will end up somewhere else.

Casey Stengel

My object in living is to unite
My vocation and my avocation
As my two eyes make one in sight

Robert Frost, 'Two Tramps at Mud-Time'*

---

*From Robert Frost. *The Collected Poems*. Vintage Classics, 2013.

ONE

TO SERVE THE COUNTRY

In 2008 I became sixty-five years old, which is considered a good time for people to retire from an active work life. My wife urged me to spend more time with her and travel to see parts of the world we had often wanted to go to but could not because I was tied up in commitments to clients. So I voluntarily retired from the Boston Consulting Group as its India chairman.

My wife and I had been living in an apartment within a golf resort in Gurgaon, near Delhi, for the previous three years. We had bought it to retire in. For my sixty-fifth birthday, she bought me a golf set to encourage me to get on the attractive greens we could see from our balcony. But, before I began playing, she took me on a trip to the graceful old European capital cities we had not visited so far—Prague and Budapest—and on a drive along the stunning Adriatic coastline in Croatia. The golf set and the greens would wait until we returned.

We took off for Prague early one morning in June 2009, shortly after the United Progressive Alliance (UPA) government was re-elected in the national elections. We checked into a little boutique hotel in the old city that evening. The next morning, when I went to shower, I realized I had forgotten to pack any underwear. We got directions to a Marks and Spencer's store, to which we proceeded after breakfast. It took me just a few minutes to buy what I wanted, whereas my wife, who had come into the store with me, wanted to look around some more. She asked me to step out and enjoy the lovely morning for a few minutes.

I stepped out and sneakily switched on my mobile phone, which I had promised would not disturb us on our long awaited holiday. There were missed calls and a message to urgently call Montek Singh Ahluwalia, who had been reappointed the deputy chairman of the Planning Commission by the prime minister, Dr Manmohan Singh.

Montek and I had been together in St Stephen's College in the 1960s. We had met very little since our college days. He had gone on to Oxford on a Rhodes scholarship (and then to the World Bank) and I had joined the Tata Administrative Services. He had returned to India and joined the government of Prime Minister Rajiv Gandhi in the 1980s, and soon after that I moved on an extended sabbatical from the Tata group to the US and to consulting. I was delighted and surprised to hear that he was trying to call me. Taking advantage of my wife's preoccupation in the store, I promptly returned his call.

'Where are you, Arun? We have been trying to reach you desperately. The prime minister wants to invite you to join the Planning Commission as a Member.'

I laughed. He seemed taken aback.

'No, seriously!' he said, 'Will you accept his invitation?'

I told him I had arrived in Prague that morning with Shama, my wife, for a holiday.

'Oh,' he paused, 'You had better ask her and decide quickly whether you will join the Planning Commission. I hope you will. May I call you in an hour?' he asked.

When Shama stepped out of the store onto the sidewalk lined with flowers into the beautiful Prague morning, she seemed delighted with the way our holiday had begun. She had found something in the store which compensated for the detour necessitated by my careless packing.

'So, what now?' she asked. I said that I had received a call saying the prime minister wanted me to join the Planning Commission. She laughed. 'Tell me another, but meanwhile let us get going to the Prague Castle.'

'No, seriously,' I said, 'what should I say to him?' I told her Montek would call again in an hour for my answer.

'Let us not spoil our holiday with all that,' she said. 'You can tell him it is a very important decision which will change the course of our lives, and you need some more time to think about it.' And we got moving to the castle.

In an hour, while we were in the castle, Montek called.

'I think you must accept the call when the prime minister calls you,' he said. 'I will suggest to his office they call you in an hour. Meanwhile please sort out with Shama what you want to do.' I told Shama what Montek said.

She said, 'You cannot talk to the prime minister here in the castle with tourists milling around. Let us quickly return to our hotel and you can take the call in the privacy of our room.' So we rushed out of the castle for transport. There were no taxis. A tram was passing by and we hopped on. Shama found a seat. I could not. I grabbed a strap as the tram swayed down the hill.

Just then my mobile phone rang: it was forty-five minutes before I was to receive the PM's call. 'This is the prime minister's office,' the caller said. 'The prime minister wishes to speak to you.'

I gulped. Dr Manmohan Singh's quiet voice came on the line. 'Arun, I would like you to join the Planning Commission and serve the country. Will you?' he asked.

I was swaying in the tram that was travelling down-hill along a curve. Hung from a strap with one hand, the phone in the other, crushed amongst tourists. 'Will you serve the country?' he had asked. No civil service examination. No pleading with any go-betweens for an opportunity. 'Yes sir!' I said.

When we got off the tram, I told my wife I had spoken to the prime minister in the tram. Tell me another, she would have laughed at another time. But something unusual was happening that day, and she asked me what he said. I told her that I had accepted his offer to serve the country as a member of the Planning Commission. 'Well, I suppose we can at least finish our holiday in peace now that that is out of the way,' she said, with the serenity to accept what one cannot change.

A few minutes later Montek called. He was delighted I had accepted. 'When will you be back,' he asked, 'so we can plan the swearing in?'

'The swearing in?' I inquired.

'Yes, you will be ranked a minister of state in the government and the prime minister will administer the oath to serve the country and the constitution.'

'Oh, oh,' I said, 'I am an American citizen technically now. I had to forego my Indian citizenship when I accepted American citizenship.'

'I forgot,' he said. 'Will you be willing to accept Indian citizenship and forego your American citizenship?'

The question took me back to the time just before my return to India in 1999 after a ten-year extended sabbatical from the Tata group. I had received a notice from the US Department of Justice that I was entitled for US citizenship. My friends in India, who were close to the Indian government, suggested I accept it. India would be very shortly allowing dual citizenship with some countries, they said, the US would be the first, and I would have the best of both worlds then. Moreover, turning down the US offer without sufficient cause would be churlish and may make it difficult to get visas to visit the US later, they said. As it turned out, the

Indian government has not yet allowed dual citizenship. I had obtained the PIO (Person of Indian Origin) card and then the OIC (Overseas Indian Citizen) card which the Indian government had introduced. They enabled me to do many things in India like any Indian. But they did not qualify me to take an oath to serve the country: for that I had to be re-admitted as an Indian citizen.

I told Montek that I would be very happy to become a full Indian citizen again and swear to serve the country. I did not know what the process for acquiring citizenship was and how long it would take. He said he would find out. It turned out to be a complicated process involving many government departments at the centre and in the state of Haryana where we lived. They were not at all familiar with the process, unlike in the US where the process of acquiring citizenship was like an assembly line in which junior government officials herded applicants along. Hardly anyone seemed to apply to become an Indian citizen. In fact, when the clerk in the office in Gurgaon heard I was applying for 'citizenship', he produced a form of application for registration as a 'senior citizen' to obtain benefits that were provided to senior citizens. His superior laughed and said to him, 'We must make him an Indian citizen before we can make him a senior citizen!'

When Montek called me a couple of days later to explain what he had learned about the process, he also told me that the prime minister was very keen that the Planning Commission be sworn in and get to work before the end of July. Shama and I decided we would have to cut short our holiday and begin the process in India for my citizenship.

Who is entitled to serve India? Whose advice can be trusted? Can advisors bringing 'foreign' ideas be good for the country? These questions had come up five years earlier when Montek was first appointed deputy chairman of the Planning Commission by Dr Manmohan Singh who became prime minister in the first UPA government. Montek had inducted a few people from international consulting companies into some committees that were set up for a mid-term appraisal of the Tenth Five Year Plan before the Planning Commission would begin formulation of the Eleventh Five Year Plan. I was appointed in a committee for small-scale industry. At that time I was the chairman of the Boston Consulting Group in India.

The Left parties in the UPA coalition, who were wary of US influence on India's policies, raised a hue and cry about 'foreigners' running India. Immediately all the other consultants voluntarily resigned. I refused to until I was asked to by the government. Rajdeep Sardesai set up a 'Big Fight' in his eponymous TV show with two Communist party leaders on one side, and an economist (with a right wing inclination) and I on the other. The question was: 'Was the government right to induct "foreign" advisors into national planning committees?'

The economist pointed out that the Communist parties were pushing foreign ideas, those of Marx and Lenin, into India. The Communist leaders said that I was beholden to a foreign company. Rajdeep prompted me to tell the audience a little about the experience I brought to the committee.

I mentioned that I had worked for the Tata group for twenty-five years, had worked hard to build industries in India, and promoted Indian companies abroad too. Rajdeep posed a question: Who was more dedicated to the improvement of India? And who did more for India—political parties or those who built industries that created jobs? I told the audience about my interview fifty years earlier with the directors of Tata Sons who were interviewing me for the Tata Administrative Service. They had told me what Mahatma Gandhi had said, that while he was fighting for India's political freedom, Jamsetji Tata had been fighting for India's economic freedom. I proudly announced that I was as patriotic as the politicians on the TV show and had as much right to serve the country when called upon to do so as they had.

On my return to Delhi, I requested a meeting with the prime minister. I thanked him for the opportunity to serve the country he had offered me. I said to him that I was a complete outsider to government, and I was not an economist. I asked him what he expected from me in the Planning Commission.

The prime minister said that India's manufacturing sector had not grown even though the licence raj had been dismantled almost eighteen years ago. Indeed, the dismantling of government control of industry was the centrepiece of the landmark economic reforms in 1991 that he was credited with. Though the economy had grown since then, especially the service sector, industry had not grown as expected. Manufacturing was still only 16 per cent of the gross domestic product (GDP) as it was before the reforms, and China had stolen a huge march over India in the meantime. Therefore, one could take the view that the economic reforms had failed to meet their principal objective, namely, the growth of industry.

He hoped that, with my hands-on knowledge of industry, I would bring in new ideas. 'We need a fresh point of view, and we need an outsider to government,' he said.

TWO

TRIPPING THROUGH RED TAPE

I reported for work in Yojana Bhavan, the imposing office of the Planning Commission on Parliament Street, a short distance from the Indian Parliament's beautiful, circular building in New Delhi. A senior officer of the Planning Commission met me accompanied by his staff. He explained to me the facilities that would be given to me so that I could 'concentrate on my work for the country,' in his words.

I would have seven personal staff attached to me—secretaries, attendants, et cetera! I could not suppress my amusement. I said, 'As chairman of the Boston Consulting Group, I shared a secretary with another officer.'

'Oh, but you will have a lot more work to do here,' he said. He went on to say that he was amused whenever he went abroad to meetings with senior government officials in so-called 'developed' countries and found that they would go to the coffee machine for their own coffee. Imagine a senior person wasting precious time making coffee, time he could have used better to address matters of vital importance to his nation! I would not have to do such trivial things myself, he declared proudly: the government of India was better organized.

Among the seven staff assigned to me, the principal duties of two were paper carrying and door opening. When I stepped out of my room for a meeting with the deputy chairman, my door was opened before I could reach it by one man who stood impassively behind it. The other tried to take my little notebook from my hand so that he could carry it for me down the corridor to the deputy chairman's meeting room. I resisted. In the corridor, I found my colleagues in the Planning Commission walking along the corridor to the meeting with their assigned paper-carriers behind them, notebooks and files in hand. When we arrived in the deputy chairman's meeting room, they sat down and their files were dutifully placed before them on the table.

When the meeting was over, I found all the paper-carriers, including my own, waiting to relieve us of our papers and notebooks. I kept mine. When I reached my office, the door was wide open waiting for me to enter, an invisible door-opening staff member standing behind it. It was a relief that I could save my mental energy for important national matters and not have to waste it to open doors! Perhaps I should have been grateful for all the help the government was giving me so that I could do my job.

The number of staff assigned to an officer, the size of the office room, and such privileges can be signals of the place of a person in a hierarchy, and private sector organizations have hierarchies too and use such signals—private parking spaces for the senior-most executives, executive washrooms, and so on. In a hierarchy-driven bureaucracy the signalling requirements of such privileges are much greater, exceeding their utility in improving efficiency. Door-openers and paper-carriers have little utility but have great signalling value. An officer who should not be expected to touch his door handle and carry his own notebook has to be a very important person.

The cherry-on-the-cake of such signalling arrangements was the revolving red beacon on the white government car I was assigned. It hardly made any difference to the speed of movement of my car in the chaotic Delhi traffic with its surfeit of cars with red beacons. Its limited utility was not the point: it was there to signal that I was an important person, which my five-year-old grandson, Viren, who visited us from New York where he lives with his parents, enjoyed greatly. He would look out of the car window and salute all the policemen we passed, though they hardly ever noticed.

My job, as the prime minister had charged me, was to develop a new strategy to grow India's manufacturing sector, using new ideas that would have to come from outside government. Time was very short. I wanted to quickly reach out to many people in industry, and to many thought leaders in India and abroad. I needed help with locating the knowledge we needed and meeting the people we should. Such assistance for networking and knowledge management was of a very different kind to the assistance for opening doors and carrying papers around that I had been generously provided with.

The Commission had many advisers, some with doctorates in their fields, who had been in the Commission and government for decades. They had experience in government. Perhaps they could help me. When I turned to them to help me bring in outsiders to work with us, they were amused by my innocence. They would have to teach me how the government worked. If I wanted to arrange a meeting in the Commission with outsiders, they would be glad to prepare a note 'on file', which I should approve. Then invitations would go out by speed post.

They seemed concerned that instead of relying on them I proposed to consult with outsiders. They had already studied these matters, they said. I offered to study whatever they could give me, but I insisted on consulting outsiders as well. What the in-house experts gave me were the same ideas that we had to break away from. Words often attributed to Albert Einstein came to my mind then, and came to me many times again as I went about the work I was expected to do in the government: 'It is madness to keep doing things the same way and expect different outcomes.'

Other new members of the Planning Commission had also been charged by the prime minister to bring in fresh thinking to the subjects they were assigned. They, too, felt handicapped by the resistance to change within the Commission. In an internal meeting of the Planning Commission's Members with the deputy chairman, Montek Ahluwalia, a request was made to allow every member to have two individuals of his or her choice from outside the Commission, or even outside government, so that new ideas could be brought in and distilled.

Files were moved to obtain the requisite government approvals to recruit these persons. The files meandered from desk to desk within the Commission, and then to other desks in other ministries whose approvals were also required — finance, personnel, and training, and so on — and back onto desks in the Commission. It seemed that within the Indian government there was still time to kill time, while outside it the country was becoming impatient for progress.

I was becoming very impatient too. I asked Montek whether he could accelerate the government's tardy approval procedures. He expressed his inability and asked me to reach out to my friends outside the government for help.

I first approached R. Gopalakrishnan, executive director of Tata Sons, who oversaw the Tata Administrative Services (TAS). I had been persuaded by the directors of Tata Sons to join the TAS forty-five years earlier when I was determined to join the government to serve the country. Here I was now in government needing the Tata group's help to do my job. Could the TAS depute a young, public-spirited officer to work with me for a year at no cost to the government? Indian industrialists were very critical of how government functioned. Here was an opportunity to help improve matters. Besides, I promised to provide a rich experience to the candidate that would exceed the TAS's requirements for developing leaders. Gopal agreed readily. I made the same request to Anand Mahindra, who also agreed. The Tata and Mahindra groups would depute young officers on sabbaticals from their companies for a year, and pay their salaries.

I interviewed the candidates from the two groups. They were released very quickly from their responsibilities within their companies because their top brass wanted to help spur industrial growth. I had found my two resources. The government would not have to pay anything, therefore no approvals would be required from it, I thought.

It is never so simple with a bureaucracy, as any viewer of the evergreen BBC serial *Yes Minister* would know. Montek thought my solution was a good idea, but wanted to be sure that no government rule was being breached. He asked the bureaucrats in the Planning Commission to check out my proposition. I was asked on what basis should a Member be seeking external assistance. I would have to follow the proper procedure to make my case for this, and only then could the question of the costs and payments if any for the assistance be considered. First things first, the bureaucrats said.

By this stage I was feeling like the man who was asked to pick up a heavy stone with his own hands. He put out his left hand, and was told, not that one. It was tied behind his back so he could not use it any more. He put out his right hand, and he was told not that either, and it too was tied.

Good bureaucrats—and there are many good ones— follow the theologian Reinhold Niebuhr's practical advice: 'God, give me the serenity to accept the things I cannot change, the courage to change the things I can, and the wisdom to know the difference.' One of these good bureaucrats in the Commission volunteered to help me.

'We have a scheme for appointing consulting organizations to do specific tasks for us,' he said. 'Why don't you describe what you want as a task to be done, and we will follow the procedure of advertising and asking for bids, and then selecting the best based on capability and cost. Fortunately, this process does not require the involvement of any other ministry and we can complete it in a month if we move the file around fast within the Commission, and I will help you with this,' he offered.

The requirement was advertised within twenty-four hours. After the stipulated two weeks, the bids would be opened and scrutinized by a committee, which I would chair, according to the governmental procedure.

My helpful and wise friend in the Planning Commission warned me that these two persons could not be hired as individuals—there was another, more complicated process for that. They would have to form themselves into a consulting company and bid as one company to take advantage of the shorter process he had recommended.

The two young officers, Sriram Ramchandran of the Mahindra group and Varoon Raghavan of the Tata group, who had never met each other before, now had to work together very quickly to overcome the first of the many governmental procedural hurdles they would encounter when they would begin their work with me. They put their heads together and formed 'Paradigm Consulting', which bid for the work. The name Paradigm came to them, they said, because they would be engaging with the government in a new paradigm of work, and were also hoping to help change other paradigms within the government.

Several bids came in, in response to the advertisement. Some were from large consulting companies, with thousands of consultants around the world. In the request for bids, it was clearly stated that the specific persons who would work full time for a year with the Commission must be named, and that the Commission would evaluate the experience and skills of these persons. Other bids were from individuals who had formed one-person consulting companies to sell their own services, many of whom were retired government officers who stated that one of their principal qualifications for the work was that they knew how the government worked.

Paradigm Consulting, whose two principals guaranteed that they would be full time with the Commission for one year, won the technical qualification round quite easily. Then came the time to open the financial bids. Sriram and Varoon proposed to do the work pro bono. They were being paid by their parent companies and they considered it unethical to ask the government to pay anything. However, my wise friend in the Commission suggested that a nil cost bid would attract too much attention. It would be best that they quote some small amount. He suggested one lakh rupees, and so they bid.

All the other bids were much higher: those from the large consulting companies very much higher, of course. Paradigm Consulting was selected. Now to work!

But where? Things are never simple in a procedure-bound bureaucracy. Only individuals paid by the Commission, as employees or as individual consultants, can be provided office space within the Commission's premises, some rule said. Since Sriram and Varoon were engaged as Paradigm Consulting, they could not be given any office space.

On the other hand, the innovative solution of creating a consulting company enabled more young people to join to help. If a consulting company, who had been awarded a contract, was willing to put additional persons to the job without charging any more, surely the client could not object! A third young person, Arjun Nath, was deputed by the Boston Consulting Group to help me shape the plan for manufacturing and industry, and joined the Paradigm team.

These young people found their own solutions for space to work. Arjun was accommodated by the Advisor for Industry in the Planning Commission within her own office. He was doing work that assisted her, she reasoned, and she needed to meet him frequently and have him work closely with her. Around that time, a director in the Industry division was assigned a larger room. When he moved out of his smaller room, he suggested that Sriram and Varoon use it until someone asked them to vacate it. So they began to use a room on the top floor of the building, a room with a desk, a chair, a large couch, and a whiteboard.

Into that room, as time went on, more young people came to work as part of an expanding Paradigm Consulting team. They had to make do with the couch, chair, and table. The whiteboard became an essential tool for them to coordinate their work together on several projects — but more about that later.

The chairman of Sona Koyo Steering, Dr Surinder Kapur, observed Sriram, Varoon, and Arjun at work supporting meetings of the industry–government joint working groups that were preparing plans for industry. He saw an opportunity to provide a leadership development opportunity for a young manager from his company while assisting the national effort to grow industry. He requested me to include Anand Seth, a young manager from Sona Koyo, in the Paradigm team on the same basis as the others. Sona Koyo would pay Anand's salary and there would be no cost to the Planning Commission. Varoon and Sriram moved back to their parent organizations and were replaced by Arjun Nohwar, another TAS officer, and Shruti Mehrotra respectively. Shikha Sharma, the chairman of Axis Bank, offered to add a person to the team on the same basis as the Tata and Mahindra groups, rotating young managers through Paradigm one year at a time, for the unusual development experience they could have while serving the nation. Later, ICICI Bank and Larsen and Toubro (L&T) also joined as partner organizations who provided young managers at no cost to the government.

Siddharth Prabhu-Coelho, a young Indian working with an investment bank in the US, wanted to take a break and do some national service. He did not expect his company to continue paying his salary, so he resigned and was prepared to work for free. Bhavana Mahajan, a postgraduate from Jawaharlal Nehru University (JNU), offered to work for free as well. Then Ajith Francis V joined Paradigm. He resigned from Google to work pro bono in the new start-up in the Planning Commission.

As the team grew, and more people had to be accommodated in the room with the one chair and couch, I requested the Planning Commission for surplus furniture elsewhere in the building to be given to them. A wise bureaucrat suggested I withdraw my official request. No one seemed to have sat up and noticed that people who were not being paid by the Commission were working within it. 'Do not bring this to anyone's notice on file,' she said, 'or they may be asked to move out altogether instead of getting the surplus furniture!'

The start-up team continued at no cost to the government. In fact, they did not even collect the one lakh rupees that was owed to Paradigm Consulting according to the contract it had won. This came to my notice when the Advisor for Industry (the one who had kindly accommodated Arjun Nath in her office earlier) proposed an innovative solution to her own staff problems two years later. The post of a file clerk in her division had been abolished and she was finding it very difficult to keep the stacks of files bound in red tape in order. She proposed to give the work on a contract basis to the clerk whose post had been abolished. She had found out that Paradigm had not collected its dues from the Commission because they did not want the money. If they were to collect it and transfer it to her division, she could engage the clerk, she said. When she suggested this to the Paradigm team, they said they did not want to bother with opening a bank account and going through all the invoicing and accounting formalities, which would make them entangled with government procedures. They wanted to concentrate on the creative work they were doing. Let the government keep the money.

An unusual, entrepreneurial start-up was growing within the government to assist me, housed out of sight, in a room with a table, chair, and couch—scarce furniture which the team shared. They set themselves up within the old world of rigid hierarchical status, with departmental silos, and assigned secretarial staff (including door-openers and paper-carriers). They were a new paradigm of organization. No hierarchy amongst them; no markers of position; no assigned resources.

THREE

A CHILD'S AMBITION

What do you want to be when you grow up? It is a question young boys are often asked. I was born on 15 August 1943 in Lahore, which was then in undivided India. This was not a question asked of girls when I was growing up. Not in India. Perhaps girls somewhere else in the world were asked this question but I was not aware of it. My world was limited to my surroundings, the people I met, what they said, and what they did.

Girls had only one way forward. They had to get married and produce children. They could be asked what sort of man they hoped to marry, or how many children they wanted to have. Or a girl may have wondered what her son could become. Her daughter surely would have no choice: she must marry and have children.

Boys would sometimes discuss what their ambitions were. To be an army general, a doctor, or a big officer in government. But only some boys, I began to realize. My boy cousins and the sons of my parents' friends would occasionally talk about their ambitions. However, I found that other boys I sometimes played with, like the gardener's or sweeper's sons, would turn quiet when I bragged about my ambitions. They knew their choices were limited by the circumstances of their birth.

I was lucky. My father, an entrepreneurial engineer, had created a very successful manufacturing business in Lahore before he was thirty years old. I realized how well off we were, some fifty years later, when I visited Lahore after he had passed away.

I looked for our house in Model Town, outside Lahore. The house was in a circle of houses around a large park, my mother had said. She described a large house, set in a large garden, with many flowering shrubs and fruit trees. My parents had cars, and also a tonga with a horse in which my mother would go into the bazaars of Lahore to shop for groceries.

I was brought by the Pakistani driver to the address my mother had given me. The entrance to the house was in front of a large, manicured park, the size of a cricket field, my mother had said. So it was, and there were men in white flannels playing cricket when I got there. My driver was confused, because instead of one gate into the house, there were two. He spoke to the guards at the gates. They said the old property had been divided and two houses had been built. In one large house, with uniformed guards at its gate, lived General Jehangir Khan. The other large house, with men in salwars lounging around, was the home of Nusrat Fateh Ali Khan, the famous Sufi singer. My father's property had been large enough for two very successful men.

On 15 August 1947, when India became independent of British rule and was partitioned into free India and Pakistan, my family became refugees. Till almost the last day it was not certain whether Lahore would be in India or Pakistan. My father, and many other Hindus and Sikhs, had hopes it would remain in India. He stayed on until it was too late. My mother, my younger brother, and I were in Shimla on the Indian side, where my mother was expecting her third child. My father came across the new national border on 15 August with just the clothes he was wearing.

He wandered a little while through the chaos of North

India following the Partition, looking for some way to support his young family: his wife and three little boys (my second brother was born in Shimla on 30 August 1947). He found employment with the Nawab of Rampur in Uttar Pradesh, to run the Nawab's engineering company, the Rampur Engineering Company. We lived in a big house, with a large garden, across from the Nawab's Palace. I was six years old by then, time to go to school. There were no English medium schools in the town, so I was sent off to a boarding school, St Mary's Convent in Nainital, a few hours from Rampur.

Two years passed quite happily. My ambition then was to be an engineer like my father. His aspiration was to rebuild the business that he had lost, and to be his own master as he had been in Lahore. When his refugee compensation came through at last, he was given a small plot of land to build a factory in a refugee rehabilitation area in Govindpuri, adjacent to the Modinagar industrial complex in western Uttar Pradesh. He resigned his job with the Nawab of Rampur and set out to build a business and a home again from scratch.

'If you can make one heap of all your winnings, and risk them on one turn of pitch and toss, and lose and start again at your beginnings, and never breathe a word about your loss...' These are lines from Rudyard Kipling's famous poem, 'If—',* which features advice to a boy about what is required to become a man. I never ever heard from my father about how we lived in Lahore, and what he had lost. I heard nostalgic snatches sometimes from my mother, and that too, rarely. Both father and mother stoically carried on as he struggled to rebuild his business. My father became a role model for me as the man from 'If—' that I wanted to be when I grew up.

Kipling came into my life too. By a combination of

---

*Rudyard Kipling. 'If—', *The Collected Poems of Rudyard Kipling.* Wordsworth, 1999.

circumstances, when my father moved from Rampur, I moved from St Mary's Convent in Nainital to the Lawrence School, Sanawar, in the Shimla Hills. 'Send him to Sanawar and make a man of him,' is the advice given for Kim,* the young orphan, in Rudyard Kipling's eponymous novel.

I would have had to move out from St Mary's whether or not my father could afford to continue paying the substantial fees of the boarding school, because the school decided they would not take boys any longer. It was a girls' convent which had been admitting young boys up to the second standard only. I am not certain why they discontinued taking boys, though Nabo, our bearer in Rampur, claimed I was responsible!

I was in the second standard, therefore amongst the oldest boys in the school. On the Annual Sports Day, I participated in a relay race in the presence of the Governor of Uttar Pradesh, many parents, and all the students—almost all of whom were girls. The race was between two boys' teams. When I took off on my leg of the relay, my belt fell open and my shorts slipped to my ankles and tripped me. My opponent whizzed past. I was intent to not let my team down, so I pulled my shorts right off to free myself to run as fast as I could to make up for lost time. The crowd began to roar in delight: I thought in appreciation of my determination to win. Afterwards, Nabo explained that the crowd was amused (and he embarrassed) because I had stripped in front of the girls. Perhaps the convent, aiming to groom prim young ladies, decided it would not take the risk any longer of the opposite sex being exposed to them too soon. So out went all the boys from school, according to Nabo.

St Mary's is for grooming ladies, Sanawar to develop men. To Sanawar then I would go. Except that my father could

---

*Rudyard Kipling. *Kim*. Macmillan & Co, 1901.

no longer afford to pay for an expensive boarding school education. Fortunately, the Government of India had recently introduced a scheme of merit scholarships for needy students. I sat for the examination and qualified.

In Sanawar, at a Founder's Day, when I was not yet a teenager, I heard the vice president of India, Dr S. Radhakrishnan, explain to the students what the tricolour flag of independent India stood for. There he stood majestically before us in his white dhoti and turban, an elbow on the lectern, one leg crossed in front of the other. 'We have to build our nation,' he said. Like a pied piper, he drew the children towards a vision he evoked. I knew then that I must serve the country when I grew up. I did not know how.

In 1959, I was admitted to St Stephen's College in Delhi to study physics. Why physics? Because the physics honours course in Delhi University was the most difficult course in the country to be admitted to then. Since I had the required high marks for admission, I must do physics, said my parents. Like a light cork without the weight of my own opinion, I was bobbed around by the views of others. Within two weeks of beginning the course, I felt I had made a mistake. Those were the Nehruvian years of nation-building. St Stephen's attracted the best of the best students from schools around the country. After they graduated, the best of them would join the civil services to serve the country. The best route to prepare for the civil services examination was to study history and economics.

So I applied to change my course, but was refused. The college principal tried to convince me that I could serve the country as well by becoming a scientist. Moreover, he said, I was too young to know what I wanted to become, and it would be best if I reflected on my future when I graduated. So I bobbed along.

The desire to serve the country remained, though I still did not know how to realize it. My views were being shaped by the opinions of the people around me. The view in the college in those years was that joining a private sector company was for losers who were not good enough to be selected into the civil services. One could make a lot more money in the private sector where starting salaries could be over Rs 750 per month, whereas the starting salary in the premier civil services was only Rs 400 per month. However, the worthiness of people was not to be judged by the amount of money they made but by the worth of the work they did. Private sector executives were pejoratively called 'box-wallahs', because they sold goods for money, like ghee (clarified butter), soap, and tea, packed in boxes. In government, in contrast, one served the country.

A job with a private sector company should have been the last thing I should have done with my aspiration to serve the country. By a strange twist of fate, after I finished my master's in physics in 1964, I ended up joining a private company, convinced that it was a very good way to fulfil my ambition to serve the country!

FOUR

A ROAD LESS TAKEN

When I finished my master's in physics, I was too young to sit for the civil services examination. Also, I had to study for some papers in other subjects on my own, since I could do only one or two papers in the sciences for the civil services examination: the rest would have to be in history or economics. Therefore, I would be at home for a year or more preparing for the examinations.

The principal of St Stephen's College had received requests from CEOs of large private companies to recommend students from the college to them. Three of these companies were in Calcutta (now Kolkata), Madras (now Chennai), and Bombay (now Mumbai). First class travel and accommodation would be provided by the companies. It was a good opportunity to see the country, especially as I had never been to Madras and Bombay before. You do not have to change your mind about sitting for the civil services examination, the principal assured me, and your knowledge of the world may be expanded by meeting senior people who you would not otherwise find it easy to meet. So I took off.

The interviews in Calcutta and Madras reinforced the stereotype of 'box-wallahs' in my mind. The interviews were one-way. The interviewers asked all the questions. They enjoyed showing off that they knew more than the interviewees. Attempts by me to ask them about what they did were suppressed as affronts to their power. I gained no new knowledge about the worthiness of their work.

The interview in Bombay was very different. It was not an interview: it was a process over three days. A small group of Tata Sons's directors engaged the interviewees in a number of exercises. Towards the end of the three days they engaged all the interviewees in an open group discussion. One of their questions was about how we had experienced the selection process. Several candidates said that they enjoyed it much more than the selection processes they had been through in other organizations. Here they had been able to talk about what *they* knew and cared about, and there were indeed a variety of things that had been discussed during those days.

The directors explained they were looking for candidates who were good learners and not the most knowledgeable people, because those they would select would be doing work they had never done before in various Tata companies: they could not be expected to already have the knowledge required. They were looking for people who were curious about the circumstances in which they were, and who were good at learning to do what they wanted to do. It could be their hobbies, or subjects they had become interested in outside their school curriculums, or student and community activities they chose to be engaged with. The selection board was not interested as much in *what* the candidates had done, as *how* they had gone about it.

The word that comes to mind is 'application'. How does this young person apply herself or himself to whatever they do? I notice I have instinctively added 'herself', though there were no women amongst the candidates. (I have mentioned this gap between the genders due to which girls in India were expected to grow up to do domestic duties. This has changed greatly now. Amongst the young team that created the entrepreneurial start-up within the government between 2012 and 2015 — the India Backbone Implementation Network — whose story I will recount later in this book, many are women.)

Back to 'application'. It is a concept associated with learning that my mother says she first encountered when I was sent off to the boarding school in Nainital. I was one of the receivers of a prize at the end of my first year. My parents were disappointed: it was not a prize for having come first in class, or first in anything, other than merely 'application'! My mother set about finding out what this was. She concluded that it was the best quality in a young person. It was their motivation to apply themselves with vigour and curiosity to whatever they were engaged with. With this, they would learn and build their own capabilities faster and better than others could.

I must say that my mother has exemplified this quality more than anyone else I have known in my life. Even in her systematic search for the significance of this new concept she encountered — application — she illustrated her own qualities of it. When my two younger brothers and I were growing up, my father was building his new enterprise in a rural area for rehabilitating refugees, away from any city. There were no cinemas, no shops, and very few other young people for company. When we would come home from our boarding schools for our long holidays, it seemed there was hardly anything interesting to do.

The word 'bored' was forbidden by my mother. How can you be bored, she would say, when there is so much to be learned about the world around you? Go out into the garden and tell me how many varieties of birds or leaves or flowers you can count. And tell me what they are. Or read a book from my library (she was a voracious reader) and tell me what new ideas you've learnt. Or make something with the tools that are lying in the attic. Or even pick up a paint brush and paint on the walls of the house! Apply yourself with vigour and curiosity to something that your circumstances enable you to have. Then you will be fully alive and never bored. This was her lesson in living.

At the end of it all, the directors met each candidate alone. When I sat before them, the chairman of the selection committee, Professor Rustum Choksi, said to me, 'Maira, we know you are preparing to sit for the civil services examination. What is your ambition in life?' I paused. An obvious answer would be to be selected for the civil services, which was very difficult and would be a great achievement (just as being selected for admission in the physics honours programme in Delhi University had been when I finished school). The committee already knew I would be sitting for the examination, so my ambition to pass the examination was not the information they were looking for. I said, 'I want to serve the country.'

'Have you considered in what ways one can serve the country?' Professor Choksi asked. Since I had not thought about this much and had been following the herd, I said, 'Yes, sir. One must join the government to serve the country.' And I left unsaid the popular view in college that working in a business organization was not about serving the country but only about making money!

Dr Jamshed Bhabha, a member of the selection committee, smiled and said, 'Maira, some of us working in industry think we serve the country too.' He had caught me out. He then went on to give me some insights from the history of the Tata group. He described the motivations of the founder of the group, Jamsetji Tata, who wanted Indians to produce steel in India with the abundant raw materials that we had. He did not want India to remain at the bottom of global supply chains in a colonial empire, in which the colonies were sources of raw materials for factories in the ruling country, who had the technology and 'added value' to the raw materials and exported their value added products around the world, including their colonies. Thus, higher value jobs were created in the ruling countries, and they became 'industrialized' and 'developed' while people in their colonies were left to dig and toil and their countries stayed undeveloped. This was the story of the cotton industry. Indians grew the cotton, but the British factories produced the cloth they became renowned for.

Jamsetji Tata set up a textile mill in Nagpur in the midst of India's cotton-growing areas. Against great odds, including obstacles created by the British, he set up the Tata Iron and Steel Company in Jamshedpur, close to large sources of iron ore and coal. He built a string of hydroelectric power plants along the Western Ghats to provide clean and inexpensive power to factories in Mumbai. He also established the Indian Institute of Science in Bangalore, and later Tatas set up the Indian Institute of Fundamental Research in Mumbai. Jamshed Bhabha then pointed out what I would quote on television many years later—that Mahatma Gandhi had said that while he was fighting for India's political freedom, Jamsetji Tata was fighting for India's economic freedom.

Professor Choksi concluded the interview by saying, 'Maira, the selection committee will be spending some time together in the next few days to decide who we will select, and even whether we will select anyone at all because we are very committed to selecting only young people with aspirations, who will be "self-starters" and learners and help us to grow Tata companies in the service of the nation. We hope that IF we make you an offer, you will consider it seriously.'

I was impressed by the Tata directors, with their selection process, and the stories of the Tata group they had told me. The possibility of receiving an offer from the Tatas caused me a great deal of emotional turmoil in the next few weeks.

Because, with this possibility, 'Two roads diverged in a yellow wood,' as the poet Robert Frost says in the opening of his poem, 'The Road Not Taken'*:

Frost goes on to say,

And sorry I could not travel both
And be one traveller, long I stood
And looked down as far as I could
To where it bent in the undergrowth;

I did pass the Tata selection test. I was made an offer, which I accepted.

Frost ends his poem with these oft-quoted words:

I shall be saying this with a sigh
Somewhere ages and ages hence:
Two roads diverged in a wood, and I—
I took the one less travelled by,
And that has made all the difference.

---

*Robert Frost. *The Collected Poems*. Vintage Classics, 2013.

FIVE

PLAYING THE INNER GAME: MAKE IN INDIA

The Tata Administrative Service was very small when I joined it in 1965. Its members were seen as a small group on a fast track to top management positions in the Tata group of companies. In the first seven years I worked on strategic issues in the Tata headquarters in Mumbai, assisting the chairmen and senior directors of the two largest companies in the group, the Tata Iron and Steel Company and the Tata Engineering and Locomotive Company, or TELCO as it was then known, which was later named Tata Motors.

Jawaharlal Nehru had formed a Planning Commission for India in 1950 to make plans for the development of the country. Independent India would need buses and trucks to move people and goods around as the country developed. The Planning Commission stated that the buses and trucks the country needed must be produced in India, so that jobs were created in the country and India could become self-reliant. Other government bodies doled out the industrial licences to produce the products the country needed. Building new industries in India was the mission of the Tata group, as the Tata directors had explained to me in my interview for the Tata Administrative Service. In 1954, with the blessings of the government, TELCO formed a joint venture with Daimler-Benz of Germany to produce that company's world-famous trucks and buses in India.

A fifteen-year technical collaboration agreement between the companies was signed. Its objective was a progressive transfer of technology from Daimler-Benz to Tatas, and the building of capabilities and jobs in India such that, by the end of the fifteen years, all the components of the trucks and buses, including the most complex ones, would be produced in India. The people in Daimler-Benz were very good teachers and the Tatas were very good learners. Within ten years the objective had been largely met. Indeed, Daimler-Benz confidently exported trucks and buses made in TELCO's factory in Jamshedpur to neighbouring countries such as Sri Lanka and Malaysia as their own products with their famous tri-cornered Mercedes star emblem proudly displayed on the bonnets. Thereby, they could reduce the costs of shipping products to these markets from their own factories in Germany.

In those heady coming-out years of the Indian nation after its Independence, there were many expressions of India's identity and its pride in itself. A song enacted by the actor, Raj Kapoor, who became famous well beyond India's borders, stated, 'My shoes are Japanese, my trousers are English, but I am Indian within.' So was the Tata truck that went abroad by the mid-1960s: all Indian inside with a German emblem outside.

The Tata directors wanted to take the next step for India's emergence as an industrial nation: to export the trucks and buses with the Tata emblem — an Indian emblem — on them rather than the Mercedes star. They also wanted to take the next step on their inner journey of learning. Indians had learned how to make trucks and buses up to the German standards. The next step was to learn how to design and engineer new products and thereby imbibe the essence of the technology, to move from Make in India to Made by India.

The German company was proud of what it had achieved.

Indeed, the Tata–Daimler joint venture was acclaimed by international development agencies at that time as the most successful transfer of technology between a developed country and an emerging economy. The next step proposed by Tatas would take the relationship into potentially more contentious territory. Tatas, the students, could emerge as competitors to their teachers in international markets where the German company was so far the most successful exporter of commercial vehicles.

The two companies agreed that, in the circumstances, the fifteen-year technical collaboration agreement, which was to end in 1969, would not be renewed. However, Daimler-Benz would remain a shareholder of the company interested in its continuing development and growth. Thus, by the late 1960s, just when I joined the Tata Administrative Service, TELCO's chief executive (and soon to be its chairman), Sumant Moolgaokar, was making plans for TELCO to set out on its own, to design, develop, and produce commercial vehicles made by Indians. Moolgaokar was building a team around himself to make and implement these plans. He pulled me in as his executive assistant, and so I sat in all his meetings and travelled with him as he went about making the dream come true.

As the plans developed, it became clear that the company would have to start a new factory away from the factory in Jamshedpur, where the first manufacturing plant had been established with German technology. The site of the new factory would be near the city of Pune (then called Poona) in Western India. The new factory would be designed and made by Indians, as would the products that would be progressively produced in it. A new research and development (R&D) centre would be required, staffed with Indians with the ambition to design Indian products. An effective programme to train young Indians would be essential to build the human assets without which the dream of 'Made in India' could not become a reality.

Moolgaokar became impatient with the planners on his team. They were focused only on the technical side of the challenge before them: the choice of machines, the layout of the workshops, and so on. No doubt these were essential. The planners were the most experienced and the best of the Indians who had worked with the Germans to build the factory in Jamshedpur. 'You are missing something,' he would say at the end of every meeting. The planners would return to their drawing boards and return with better plans. Moolgaokar, while appreciating the refinements, would nevertheless end with the observation that something was amiss. Like the students of the Zen Master, who become tired with trying to find the answer to the koan (an unsolvable puzzle) he gives them, the planners became exhausted and asked Moolgaokar what they were missing.

'Human beings,' said Moolgaokar. 'Who is going to run all these machines you are putting in your plans? Who is going to design and make them—and we will have to make them ourselves because the country does not have the foreign exchange to import them? Who is going to design and test the parts of the new trucks that will be made on these machines? Who are these people going to be? Where will they come from? What will enable them to acquire skills they do not have and learn work they may never have done before?' Then he turned to me and changed my life forever.

'It is clear, gentlemen, that none of you can nor should unlearn what you have learned very well, which is the creation of the technical side of an enterprise. We need someone who can learn something that will be very new to all of us: the creation of the human side of an enterprise from scratch. So I am giving this important task to young Maira here, who is the youngest and most innocent amongst us. And time is very short. We must have the people even before the machines.'

He set me to learn something very new to me (and to the

organization too), which was the creation of an institutional ability to attract, motivate, and enable large numbers of people to learn very fast to do what they do not know how to do. On our own we had to create a new industrial enterprise that would compete against the best of the best in the world including our erstwhile teachers, Daimler-Benz. For the first few years I continued to work on the company's new manpower plans from the headquarters in Mumbai, close to Sumant Moolgaokar, while travelling around the country to the Indian Institutes of Technology, the Industrial Training Institutes, and the new Indian Institutes of Management to source the best-of-the-best of Indian talent. Then, in 1973, by when the new factory in Pune had acquired some physical shape, Moolgaokar transferred me there to 'get to the ground, rub my nose on the shop-floor, and build the people along with the people,' he said.

I was only thirty years old then. My transfer to Pune was with a substantial promotion as the number two man in the organizational hierarchy, over the heads of others, with many years of experience in Jamshedpur, and some as old as my father. My appointment did not go entirely well with them, and least well with my new boss, Sharad Jakatdar, who was the senior-most of them. He thought I was an upstart, and, perhaps, an undeserving one. While he and his colleagues had earned their positions through hard work, in his mind I was part of the undeserving elite who were privileged because they belonged to the right families and went to the best universities. Indeed, the Tata Administrative Service until then had mostly hired Indians who had graduated from Oxford or Cambridge, like the old Indian Civil Service (ICS). I was one of the very few exceptions. But Jakatdar did not know this yet.

Jakatdar was a fiery patriot from Nagpur in central India. He had trained with the Rashtriya Swayamsevak Sangh (RSS) when he was a teenager and joined a guerrilla gang fighting the British in India. He was arrested and imprisoned for being involved in a plot to blow up a railway line. In Jamshedpur he was an outsider to the elite social circle of golf-playing officers and their wives. He thought I was one of those. Moreover, my being picked by Moolgaokar to do something very important that he and the others had proven they could not do while making the plans—an indication that they had failed and I could be better than them—did not sit well with him.

He gave me a very frosty reception when I reported for duty in his office in Pune. He sucked on his pipe and observed me through the smoke for a minute.

'I presume you play golf,' he said.

'No, sir,' I said.

He paused and asked slowly, 'You have never played golf?' I admitted my failing, I had not. Then he tapped his pipe in an ash-tray and put it down. He asked me where I had studied, and wanted to know my family's history. Having heard it, he concluded, 'You are different.' He seemed to warm up to me. (For the record, he and I developed a great working relationship. We complemented each other: he on the technical side of the enterprise, I on its human side; and we wove the fabric of the institution together.)

He shared his dreams for the enterprise in Pune. He ended the meeting saying, 'Maira, I am glad you do not play golf. If I catch you playing golf, I will know that you think your work is done and it is time to play golf. The truth is we have so much to do to build our country and so little time. There cannot be any time for golf. So don't let me see you on a golf course!'

He made an indelible mark on me. Since then, whenever I have been tempted to consider golf, a nagging guilt arises in me and I ask myself what I am leaving unfinished.

Moolgaokar's vision and Jakatdar's drive propelled me, and the results of our efforts became visible quite soon. They were even noticed by a prescient observer, V.S. Naipaul, the Nobel Prize winner for literature who has written several books about India, the country of his ancestors. The first of these was *India: An Area of Darkness* in which he laments India's being stuck in its past. In the next one, *India: A Wounded Civilization*, written in 1977, he despairs at the slow pace of change in the country. In this book there is only one page with a clear ray of hope. This is his account of his visit to the TELCO factory in Pune where I had been transferred by Moolgaokar. Naipaul writes:

'The plateau around Poona is now in parts like a new country, a new continent. It provides uncluttered space, and space is what the factory-builders and machine-makers say they need: they say they are building for the twenty-first century. Their confidence, in the general doubt, is staggering. But it is so in India: the doers are always enthusiastic. And industrial India is a world away from the India of bureaucrats and journalists and theoreticians. The men who make and use machines – and the industrial revolution is increasingly Indian: more and more of the machines are made in India – glory in their new skills... An industrial job in India is more than just a job. Men handling new machines, exercising technical skills that to them are new, can also discover themselves as men, as individuals.'

The factory in Pune must be 'a learning factory,' Moolgaokar would keep reminding me. 'Every person in the factory, from the general manager to the gardener, must keep learning,' he said. On his frequent visits to the factory he would ask whomsoever he encountered, including the gardener, what was different in whatever they were doing from the last time he had talked with them. He kept prodding everyone to learn and innovate. 'Something new from everyone' was his motto for the learning factory.

I often recall a passage from the acceptance speech Sumant

Moolgaokar gave when he was awarded the prestigious Sir Jehangir Gandhy Medal for Industrial Peace. He said:

'The key to bringing out the best from men is to expect the best from them. Our people do respond to this demand for the best and set standards which people seem to, somehow, find surprising in India. There is this belief, even amongst leaders of men in our country, that our culture and our Indian character cannot allow our people to attain consistent high standards, that shoddiness and carelessness are our god-given, unalterable way of life. But, if with faith in them, you ask our men for the best, they rise to your belief in their worth and create a momentum towards improvement that results in high standards in everything they do. Often have I seen the men who are considered ordinary rise to extraordinary heights. Do not accept second-rate work: expect the best, ask for it, pursue it relentlessly and you will get it.'

(He gave this speech in 1984 when it was still politically correct to refer to 'men' whenever one talked about people. He was a great believer in the capability of women too.)

When Moolgaokar unexpectedly promoted me to become the number two person in the Pune factory over many older and more experienced people than myself, I had expressed my inadequacy to him.

'How can I guide these persons who know more than me?' I asked.

'Don't try to teach them,' he said. 'Concentrate on learning from them and from everyone.' He prodded everyone with questions, and he would prod me too whenever we met. 'What have you learned? Is there something new you are doing?' He was particularly interested in innovations I was bringing about in approaches to develop people.

We conceived an entirely new architecture for managing the performance of workmen. They would be compensated according to how much useful knowledge and skills they had, and not according to how much they produced. How much they could produce would be affected by sales demands, timely supply of materials, and other factors beyond their control, whereas their desire to improve their skills and their application to learn was within them. The company would provide them opportunities to work on new machines, challenge them to do more complicated tasks, and provide them training on their own time. If they learned to do these new tasks at satisfactory levels of quality and responsibility, they would be paid higher salaries.

This method of paying for skills rather than output made the introduction of new processes and new products much easier than in the traditional system of paying for output. In that system, there would be disputes about what the standard rate of production should be. Workers would resist moving from less to more complicated work because it would be difficult to produce the same volume of output. Thus the factory as a whole would become less innovative, and it would be a slow learner because there would be resistance to change and to the introduction of new processes and products. The new system in Pune worked very well. As V.S. Naipaul observed, the young workmen in Pune gloried in their new skills.

SIX

MADE BY INDIA:
DAVID TAKES ON GOLIATHS

One day in January 1977, I went to the company head office in Mumbai to get the chairman's endorsement for changes in the wage system in Pune. I found him with the deputy chairman of the company, Mr Nani Palkhivala, (who was also the country's most famous constitutional lawyer then), surrounded by the top executives of the company. There had been a crisis the previous day.

Our company had entered into a joint venture two years earlier with a Malaysian company to set up a factory to make trucks and buses in Malaysia. Malaysia had gained its independence from the British Empire in 1957, ten years after India got its independence. Like India, it also embarked on a programme of industrial development. And, like India, it too, encouraged joint ventures between domestic companies and foreign companies who had the required technologies. Licences were handed out by the government to selected parties, as India had done before. A Malaysian prince obtained one of these licences to set up a company in partnership with Tatas. Licences had already been given to others, mostly locally established companies owned by Malaysian–Chinese businessmen in joint ventures with European and Japanese truck companies whose products these local companies had been importing into Malaysia earlier.

The Malaysian prince obtained the licence on the grounds that Malaysia should have at least one company owned and run by a 'bumiputra' (son of the soil), that is, a native Malay. Malaysia had a national 'bumiputra' policy to rectify the historical dominance of ethnic Chinese in the Malaysian economy. By this policy, positions in the government and places in universities would be reserved for Malays, and Malays would also be given preference for industrial licences if they could come up with viable propositions.

The Malaysian prince, Tengku Arif Bendahara (who was the younger brother of the Sultan of Pahang who became King of Malaysia a few years later), invited the Tata group to be his partner in the truck manufacturing venture. He appealed to Tatas, who had a history of building Indian owned and managed industrial capabilities, to support nation-building efforts in Malaysia and to help the historical under-dogs, the bumiputras. Moreover, he pointed out, Daimler-Benz, Tatas' partners in India, had been successfully selling trucks and buses in Malaysia, with their brand name and the famous Mercedes star on the grill, that were made in the Tata factory in Jamshedpur (because the shipping distance from India to Malaysia was much less than from their factories in Germany).

'Make and sell trucks in Malaysia with your own Indian brand name and logo,' he urged. 'Show the world that India can do it too!' Commercially, the venture made no sense for Tatas. The waiting list for Tata trucks and buses in India was as long as seven years! The growth of the Indian economy had created a huge demand for commercial vehicles. Supply could not keep up. The Tata group did not have to advertise their products. The company was well known and much in demand in India. Tatas had been exporting some trucks and buses to neighbouring countries, such as Sri Lanka, where European products were also sold, to test their products against competition with a view to continuously improve the trucks and buses produced and sold in India.

Though Tengku Arif Bendahara's proposition made little commercial sense for Tatas at that time, he triggered the Tata directors' super-ordinate aspirations to build India—its capabilities and its image in the world—that had inspired the Group's founder to set up the steel plant in Jamshedpur in the teeth of the British Indian government's opposition.

'Just give us the technology,' Tengku urged. 'Send some technical managers to set up and run the plant. My people will manage the finance, sales, and administration.' There was a model for this arrangement in the very successful joint venture that Daimler-Benz and the Tata group had formed in 1954, whereby the Tatas built capabilities to produce trucks and buses. Daimler-Benz had provided the technology and sent technical staff. The Tata group managed the finances, sales, and administration. On the same lines, a joint venture company was formed between Tengku and Tatas in Malaysia in 1975, named Tatab Industries (a neat amalgamation of 'Tata' for Tata, and 'Tab' for Tengku Arif Bendahara).

The Tatab joint venture did not work out the way the earlier joint venture with Daimler Benz in India had. Whereas the Tatas had been building and running successful companies in India for over fifty years before the joint venture with Daimler-Benz, and therefore had good capabilities to manage finances, distribution networks, and administration in India, Tengku and his associates had no previous experience in creating and running industrial enterprises. Moreover, the Tata brand name, though a household name in India, was completely unknown in Malaysia. Meanwhile, the other joint ventures in Malaysia were progressing well, run by Chinese entrepreneurs with experience in business, selling internationally well-known brands already trusted in Malaysia, such as Ford, Bedford, Volvo, Nissan, Mitsubishi, and, above all, Mercedes Benz, the market leader.

Two underdogs had come together in Tatab to fight with combinations of much larger and better established organizations. It was a greatly unequal contest and Tatab was soon bleeding.

The Arab–Malaysian Bank that had given Tatab a loan to set up the company realized that they were in a losing game and informed Tengku and Tatas that the bank had decided to pull out. The emergency meeting at the Tata headquarters in Mumbai, which I became an observer of, was to take stock of the crisis and determine what should be done.

The Tata group's hands were tied. Those were years of great foreign exchange shortages for India and stringent foreign exchange controls. Indian government restrictions prevented Tatas from sending any money to Malaysia to support the venture. At the same time, for its own political compulsions, the Malaysian government's rules required that the company be managed by bumiputras. The failure of Tatab would be a blow not only to the Tata group but also to the Malaysian government's policy.

There was an agreement in the meeting in Mumbai that there had been a failure of management, which was the responsibility of the Malaysian partner. However, Tatas would not escape a blow to their reputation and to the image of India. The only way out could be for Tatas to be given a chance to manage Tatab and turn it around. Perhaps the Malaysian government could be persuaded to make an exception to its policy and save the only bumiputra company in the industry. A decision was taken and a message was drafted to Tengku and the Arab–Malaysian Bank saying that Tatas were prepared to manage the company if permitted to turn it around and save the bank from losses.

Then Mr Moolgaokar got down to the brass tacks. 'Which one of you is prepared to go to Malaysia and turn the company around?' he asked all the senior executives present. There were no volunteers, nor could anyone be persuaded. Sitting quietly, I began to feel déjà vu. It turned out as I apprehended. Just as he had many years earlier, when he unexpectedly chose me to find a solution for the company's requirements of human assets for its growth, he surprised everyone by pointing to me. 'Maira will be our man in Malaysia,' he declared.

SEVEN

NO TIME TO KILL TIME

In a few days I was on an aeroplane to Malaysia, a country I did not know, and had had no need to until then. I found a few books to read about Malaysia, one of which, *The Soul of Malaya*,* I was reading while the aeroplane flew over the Indian Ocean. *The Soul of Malaya* is a beautiful description of Malaya (as Malaysia used to be known before its Independence), written by the Frenchman Henri Fauconnier. Each chapter describes a facet of the country which Fauconnier had grown to love, and each chapter begins with a phrase to set if off. One of these is 'Malaya: Where there is still time to kill time.'

The Arab–Malaysian Bank agreed to give Tatab three more years to turn a profit, and the Malaysian government agreed to permit a non-bumiputra to be the CEO of the company for three years only. I knew there would not be much time for me to kill in Malaysia.

In my first meeting with the Tatab Board in Kuala Lumpur, I was given two propositions, both of which I turned down. One was to fire the entire executive team, because, according to the Board, they were all incompetent and responsible for the company's problems. The other was a Board resolution proposing that Tatab become a corporate member of the Royal Selangor Golf Club. This would enable the CEO to play golf

---

* Henri, Fauconnier. *The Soul of Malaya*. Diddier Millet, 2007.

regularly, the resolution stated, and playing golf with the elite of Kuala Lumpur would be a good way for the CEO to promote sales of the company's trucks and buses.

When I read the resolution, the warning given to me by Mr Jakatdar when I reported for work in Pune flashed through my mind. 'If I ever find you on the golf course, I will know that you think you have time because you think your work is done. But your work will not be done.' I told the Board that I would like a few days to understand what the problems of the company were and what needed to be done. Then I would decide for myself what I should do with the executive team and whether playing golf was a good idea.

Golf, it is widely held, is a game one plays with oneself. The effortless drives and calm putts with which masters get the little ball to go where they want it to are the results of the practice of getting their arms, legs, and bodies to do what they should to make the ball go where their eyes have set the goal. They master the inner game of golf and thus they win the outer game.

The role of the inner game in winning the outer game was eloquently expressed 2,300 years ago by a young man of age sixteen. Alexander said to his tutor and biographer, Eumenes, 'The gods put dreams into the hearts of men—dreams, desires and aspirations that are often much bigger than they are. The greatness of a man corresponds to the painful discrepancy between the goal he sets for himself and the strength nature granted him when he came into the world.'

Alexander was dreaming of conquering the whole world and reaching the ends of it—in fabled India. It was an audacious goal for a young prince in Macedonia, who would have to contend with the Greek city-states to begin with, and then the mighty Persian Empire beyond, and after that, across the mountains, to India with its kings and their powerful armies and mighty elephants. Alexander died very young, when he was thirty-three, but he had achieved his dream and was known thereafter as Alexander the Great. Alexander at sixteen was acutely aware of 'the painful discrepancy' that he must overcome by disciplining himself and building his own abilities so that he could realize his dreams.

The outward, stated goal of my mission in Malaysia was to make Tatab earn a profit in three years. I had to very quickly assemble a team that was competent to achieve this goal. What must be the strategy to beat the established and much stronger competition? Therefore, what competencies must the team have? Would I find people with these competencies in Malaysia, a country I did not know at all? Could the present team develop the competencies required and very quickly overcome their 'painful discrepancy'?

While I was struggling with these very difficult questions, I began to realize I had a much bigger goal I wanted to achieve than enabling Tatab to meet its profit objectives. I sensed very acutely that Indians were generally looked down upon in Malaysia when compared to people from other countries. People in Malaysia were dismissive of India: it was a backward country compared to the countries in the West and Japan. Managers from the West and Japan knew how to get things done efficiently: Indians did not. The travails of Tatab in Malaysia was glaring evidence of this to people in Malaysia. Enterprises in Malaysia 'made by' Western and Japanese companies worked well: an enterprise made by an Indian company—even the Tatas, the very best—did not work and could not compete with the others. To admit that the management of Tatab was actually in bumiputra hands while the management of the other companies was by mostly local Chinese, was politically incendiary and was hidden even by the bumiputra managers of Tatab. It suited them to deflect the blame onto the Indians.

The superordinate goal that grew in my heart was to prove

that Indian management could be the best in the world. In my conversations with the members of the Tatab executive team, who the Board wanted me to fire, I recognized that all of them had deep desires to prove that they were very worthy people.

For the Indian technical managers who had been deputed by Tatas to Malaysia, the desire to 'save face' and build a good reputation for India and Tatas was easily evoked. Tatab's sales manager was a local Chinese executive, who had been successful with an MNC automobile company earlier and switched to Tatab because he wanted the challenge of building a new brand. Since the company's financial problems were a result of poor sales, he was the principal target of blame from the Board, and from the Indians too. He, in self-defence, blamed the Indians for the poor quality of the products, inadequate spare parts, and the training of service personnel — the technical inputs that Tatas were expected to provide.

The in-fighting within the executive group had become vicious. When I landed in Malaysia, I was told that Tatab's spare parts and service manager, a senior executive deputed by Tatas, had found his pet dog strangled on his doorstep one morning. He feared that the Chinese sales manager had commissioned some Chinese underworld gangs to do it.

I needed to very quickly learn the Malaysian market for trucks and buses. Who were the real buyers? What did they want? How could they be convinced to buy a Tata product? (Would I expect to meet them in the Royal Selangor Golf Club, for example? And would playing a round of golf with them convince them to switch from buying Mercedes trucks to Tata trucks?)

I asked the sales manager to introduce me to buyers of trucks and buses and take me along with him on his sales drives so that I could learn about the market. My desire to learn before judging seemed to warm him to me, and he began to reveal his own aspirations. He was a very proud and determined man. He feared he had lost the respect of his peers — professionals in automobile marketing, and more than that, of the Chinese businessmen who dominated the business of buying and operating trucks and buses in Malaysia. What he wanted, most of all, was to 'save face' (a common Chinese expression) and to prove to them that he was the best of the best amongst them.

We ate breakfasts together of quail eggs and Chinese porridge in roadside food stalls in the interior of Malaysia, far from the Royal Selangor Golf Club, as we travelled together to meet the real operators and buyers of trucks. We got to know each other, and realized that we had a shared aspiration, which was to prove to those who doubted us that we, the underdogs, were as good as they were, perhaps even better.

Tatab's finance manager was a Malaysian of Indian origin. While he had pointed out the mismanagement of the company, which was his professional responsibility and which led to the existential crisis for the company, he was pained that a company associated with India was seen as a failure. It hurt his own identity.

Tatab's administration manager was a Malay — a bumiputra, as was required under the Malaysian law. He was a very gentle man. He was sad that the problems of Tatab were being cited as an example of the incompetence of Malays. He dearly wanted Malays to prove that they were as good as the rest, and therefore, he wanted Tatab to succeed.

The deep aspiration that united the entire team in Tatab was a superordinate goal. Everyone wanted to prove that they and their community or country were worthy of respect. We realized that none of us could achieve this aspirational goal alone. We must work together. We had to beat the competition to prove we were equal to, and even better than the best. Only by trusting each other and by collaborating more effectively could we beat better endowed competitors. We would stop the blame game for the past. We would create the future we all wanted together.

I informed the Board that no one in the executive team would be replaced. I also informed it that playing golf at the Royal Selangor Golf Club was a waste of precious time. We would meet the bankers' and the Malaysian government's tight deadlines and we did not have any time to waste. In my brief sojourn in Malaysia, into which Fauconnier's Malaya was transforming, there would be no time to kill time.

A shared, superordinate aspiration can convert a bunch of competing and contentious individuals into a powerful, unified team. Their shared aspiration is the magnet that brings their energies into alignment. It draws them to stretch together towards a shared dream that the gods put in their hearts, and bridge the 'painful discrepancy' that Alexander the Great pointed to between what they desire and the capability they have when they begin their eventful journey to their goal.

The 'inside journeys' of each of the Tatab team, and their support to each other, enabled them to achieve the external results asked of them. Within a short eighteen months, sales of Tata trucks and buses exceeded the sales of all other companies in Malaysia and at prices higher than everyone else except the premium Mercedes Benz. More sales and higher prices enabled Tatab to become profitable within two years, ahead even of the tight three-year deadline the bankers had set.

Many innovations in the management of sales, service, distribution, and production enabled the Tatab team to achieve its remarkable results. Such innovations are induced by a 'creative tension', the term that Robert Fritz (author of *Path of Least Resistance,* published by Random House, 1984) has used to describe the spirit that drives great artists and great inventors to produce innovations. It is the tension between the outcome they want to create and their current reality: the sound of music they hear in their ear that they want to reproduce and the sound they actually produce. They will not rest until they have learned to produce the sound they want to hear.

Lim Tek Pan, the sales manager, his team of salesmen, and I worked out a sales strategy to overtake Mercedes-Benz, the market leader. The Malaysian economy was growing fast; roads were being built; transportation was increasing; most buyers of trucks were small, hardworking Chinese businessmen.

Chinese business people would say with pride that they were 'practical' people. They often made fun of the Malays who were impractical, loved pomp and show, and made bad businessmen, according to the Chinese. The Chinese worked hard in the day driving their trucks. (They had no time to play golf!) They liked to enjoy their evenings, drinking good brandy and feasting with their families, and they aspired to own Mercedes cars. We noticed that they bought Mercedes trucks, with the famous three-point star on the grille, but drove Toyota cars because they could not afford a Mercedes car.

We developed a sales proposition for these 'practical' Chinese businessmen. Show them a comparison of the Tata and Mercedes trucks. Tell them the Tata truck had the Mercedes heritage and its guts were as strong. Compare the prices of the two, and also their operating costs—the Tata trucks were more economical. Show them the calculation that if they bought a Tata truck, then within a year they could afford a Mercedes car. 'If you are a practical person, you would not pay so much more just to have a fancy star on your truck, which is your workhorse. You should have the star on the car in which you drive your girlfriend and family in the evening.' The Tatab salesmen would assure Chinese truck buyers that if they bought a Tata truck, then within a year they would own a Mercedes car. It worked. Those who bought Tata trucks were able to show off their new Mercedes cars to Mercedes truck owners who were still driving Toyota cars!

Trucks, unlike cars, are means of earning livelihoods. If they are out of operation, it is not merely an inconvenience, it also affects incomes. Deepak Rai, the service and spare parts manager, and his team ensured that Tata trucks would never be out operation. The service centres of all companies in Malaysia closed on weekends. If a Mercedes, or any other companies' truck had a breakdown on a Saturday, it would have to wait until Monday. Meanwhile the operator could not earn any money. In this scenario, we made sure the owner of a Tata truck could get emergency service over the weekend as well.

Deepak Rai became a legend in Malaysian truck circles. One night he received a call that a Tata truck carrying fish to Kuala Lumpur had broken an axle shaft fifty miles out of town. The fish would rot if the truck did not reach the market before the morning. Deepak, who was fifty years old, drove to the parts' warehouse, picked up an axle shaft, and himself drove in the night to the broken down truck on the highway. Once he was there, he slid under the truck and, with the help of the driver and some others, he replaced the shaft. The fish reached the market by the morning. The story of the Tatab service manager's commitment to customers spread around.

Since all the truck manufacturers in Malaysia imported completely knocked down (CKD) packs and spare parts from their parent companies in Europe, Japan, and India, often a spare part would not be immediately available due to shipping delays. Tatab's policy in Malaysia was that, in such a situation, the part would be taken out of a CKD pack and given to the customer. This would cripple the production of a new truck and Tatab would not be able to get the income from its sale. But the truck operator's income would not be affected. The

Tatab policy was that we had no business to put another truck on the road when we could not look after those already operating.

The word-of-mouth story amongst truck operators in Malaysia was that Tata managers cared that their customers should make money, whereas managers of other companies cared about making money for their companies. Tata truck owners benefited and drove Mercedes cars! It became easy to sell Tata trucks, and soon sales of Tata trucks overtook all others.

Thus, driven by a deeply felt, shared aspiration, the Tatab managers worked as a great team, and produced the results required within two years, not three. They overcame the 'painful discrepancy' they had felt as the underdogs when they took up the challenge. The Tata management back in India decided that I should come home to Pune to continue the journey I was on to build an enterprise in India made by Indians that would make India proud.

Just before I left, I received an invitation from the Japanese CEO of the Toyota joint venture in Malaysia to assemble and sell trucks and buses made by Hino (a Toyota subsidiary). The Japanese had a strong reputation for good quality and good management. They sold products at prices lower than everyone. They were formidable competitors. They had come to Malaysia before Tatas and their sales were increasing rapidly. Yet Tatab beat them. The CEO wanted to meet me to congratulate me, and he said he would be glad if I brought along the team of Indian managers who had worked with me.

This was at very short notice. The only Indian manager I could take with me was Deepak Rai, the service and spare parts manager. The other three Indian managers were in the factory many hours away from Kuala Lumpur. The Japanese CEO was accompanied by five Japanese managers. Over tea, he congratulated me for Tatab's performance. He commented on how immature local Malaysian managers were. He was sure that there were lots of expatriate Indian managers to explain Tatab's success and asked how many we were. I said, 'Five.' 'No, not in your office, Mairasan, in the whole company?' he asked. I repeated my answer. He paused in awe, and then stood up and bowed, his Japanese colleagues with him. 'We are twenty Japanese altogether in my company. You five Indians have beaten us. Mairasan, one Indian equals five Japanese!' he said.

The recognition that Indians were not lesser managers than those from any other part of the globe was the aspirational goal I had set out to achieve with my expatriate Indian teammates. We achieved our goal because our Chinese, Malay, and Malaysian Indian colleagues were on their inner journeys too, to achieve their goals of respect for themselves and their communities. Together we achieved our shared aspirations.

EIGHT

AN INNOVATIVE ENTERPRISE

I returned to India to take on responsibility for all TELCO operations in Pune, including divisions to design and make the machine tools and production equipment the company needed for producing new models of vehicles, and for expanding its production. The Japanese companies arrived in India soon after. They were formidable competitors and were conquering markets in many parts of the world including North America, Europe, and Asia. When the Indian government relaxed some industrial licensing laws, thus opening a chink in the Indian market to foreign companies in the 1980s, the first to come in were four Japanese companies: Toyota, Nissan, Mitsubishi, and Mazda. They were permitted to assemble and sell light commercial vehicles in India.

Those were still the days of industrial licensing in India. The government handed out permissions to companies which stated what and how much they could produce. Tatas were licensed to produce commercial vehicles only above an 8-tonne gross vehicle weight. The company had never been permitted to make lighter vehicles, even though there was a growing demand for them and the Indian manufacturers who had been licensed to produce them could not meet the requirements. The Japanese companies (with their Indian partners) were given licences to produce vehicles below an 8-tonne gross weight for this growing market segment. They were permitted to import the parts from Japan and assemble the vehicles in India with a promise to progressively produce parts in the country in a 'phased manufacturing programme'.

TELCO asked the government for permission to make light commercial vehicles too. It was denied on the grounds that the four Japanese joint ventures would have enough capability. TELCO persisted because the light segment was the fastest growing segment, and if TELCO was shut out of this, the Japanese companies could grow very large in the market and begin to dominate distribution channels. Moreover, if the government continued to open markets further, as it seemed now inclined to do, the Japanese would enter into markets for vehicles above 8 tonnes too. It was strategically imperative for TELCO to enter into the market for light commercial vehicles in India very soon and face the Japanese head-on.

Thus, another fight between TELCO and the Japanese companies was imminent. The last one was in a foreign country. This one was in India. While TELCO had the advantage of knowing its own terrain, its great disadvantage was that it did not have any light commercial vehicle products to compete with the Japanese. TELCO would have to develop them from scratch. Of course, this was provided the Indian government gave permission to an Indian company to compete with foreign companies in India itself!

The government dithered. There was no more foreign exchange available for the commercial vehicle sector. The quota for the import of parts and technology had been exhausted by the four Japanese joint ventures. If TELCO wanted to enter the light commercial vehicle market, the government ruled that TELCO would not be allowed to import either technology or parts. The products would have to be designed in India and all parts would have to be made in India. The company decided to take up the challenge. It had set up a vehicle design and development centre in Pune and it had capabilities to design and make the machines and tools required to produce the parts as well.

The problem was the very limited time available. By the time the Indian government gave the permission to TELCO to proceed, the Japanese companies were already signing up dealers and selling some vehicles in the country. Their products were making a very good impression, as they had in other parts of the world where they had already acquired large market shares. The strategy and marketing executives in our headquarters said we only had two years to have a product that could beat the Japanese in dealers' show rooms.

This seemed impossible. Designing, testing, tooling up, and producing a new vehicle is a complicated process and takes a long time. New product development times for German and American companies were above five years. The Japanese, who were the fastest, took three to four years. How could TELCO do it in less than two years?

This was the challenge for the TELCO team. Clearly, once again, the TELCO team would have no time to kill time, and nor would any in the team have time to play golf!

I remember the meeting of the managers in Pune when we received the news that, at last, the government had permitted us to compete with the Japanese on the condition that we would have to rely only on our own skills and wits—no import of technology, no import of parts.

The challenge was audacious. The meeting became playful. Someone recalled President John F. Kennedy's call for America to put a man on the moon in ten years to beat the Soviets, who had stolen a march in the space race. It had not seemed possible at all, yet America had done it. Someone else mentioned that General Motors was working on a massive project to develop new models of small cars to beat the Japanese in America, and this was called Project Saturn. Then someone came up with the idea that we should launch a project to develop a light commercial vehicle to beat the Japanese, and that we should call it Project Jupiter! Why Jupiter, someone else asked? Oh, because Jupiter is bigger than Saturn! And it is a more benevolent planet than Saturn, explained another, who had an astrological bent of mind.

'Why should we make the deadline for Project Jupiter eighteen months, and not the two years we seem to have,' asked another? 'We have no idea so far how to do it in eighteen months or in two years,' was the playful reply, 'so let us see what it would take to do it in eighteen months.'

In that playful, creative mode, more questions were asked. 'Can't we re-engineer the conventional product development process? Why does it take so long to develop a product? What are avoidable wastes of time?'

The team drew up an overall project plan compressed into eighteen months. The development process has to proceed in steps from design to product testing to pre-production and process testing and through further steps to production. Each step requires resources and they are limited. What if all the departments put resources together for each stage, and thus increased the resources available to the company for every step?

Another benefit of pooling resources and enabling cooperation in every step would be the breaking down of departmental silos. This would reduce the finger-pointing and passing of the buck that usually causes much friction and loss of time in the product development processes. Each department 'throws the brick over the wall' to the next one. For example, the design is sent to the manufacturing engineering group, who find faults with the design and throw it back over the wall and ask for changes in the design; and so on in all the serial steps.

In the 1970s, while TELCO was setting up a large new factory in Pune, independent of its teacher of technology,

Daimler-Benz of Germany, the country began to face severe shortages of foreign exchange. Imports of machines were severely curtailed and the Government of India decided to set up a government-controlled company, Hindustan Machine Tools (HMT), to make the machines that Indian companies would need. TELCO's requirements of special purpose machines that would be required for automobile production were very large. HMT was a novice and had very little capacity. TELCO's expansion would be in jeopardy if it relied on HMT. The company obtained the government's permission to make special purpose machines for itself (and also precision tools and dies). Machine tools and dies embody the technology of production. They are specialized fields and very few automobile producers in the world make their own machines and dies: they rely on specialist firms from whom they buy them. Not even Daimler-Benz makes the special machines and dies it uses in its factories in Germany and elsewhere. With the decision to be self-supporting, TELCO ventured into new and deeper areas of technology.

By the late 1970s, computer-numerically-controlled (CNC) machines were being developed in Japan. CNC machines were expensive, and could produce small volumes only, but they provided great flexibility to product designers and factory managers. Since TELCO's strategy was to hereafter design its own products, and since TELCO's volumes of production would be much smaller than the large European, American, and Japanese producers, the company decided to learn how to make CNC machines and signed technology purchase agreements with two leading Japanese CNC machine producers. TELCO had begun to use some of its own-made CNC machines in Pune when Project Jupiter was conceived.

Sumant Moolgaokar had the vision to build 'learning factories'. An innovative human resource management (HR) architecture had been introduced in the Pune factories that stimulated rapid upgradation of the skills of workmen. Workmen's salaries were increased as soon as they could establish, through objective tests, that they could operate at a higher level of skill in their trade, or that they had learned another trade at the same level of skill and were thereby increasing their versatility. Thus a grinder with level three skills could earn more money if he could operate a grinding machine at level four, or if he learned to operate a milling machine at level three. The company provided training programmes the workmen could avail of on their own time. Moreover, they did not have to wait for vacancies in higher grades or other posts. The only constraints on the accelerated learning process were an objective test of skills, and an interval of two years before a workman could apply for another skill or versatility test. Some motivated workmen had reached the highest levels of skills in multiple trades. They were designated as Master Craftsmen. They wore special uniforms and were highly respected by everyone. They were the human equivalent of CNC machines with an added advantage: they could imagine what was required and then use their range of skills to produce it.

This innovative learning system increased the skills available in the workforce tremendously. It was up to the management now to use their capabilities strategically. An opportunity came with Project Jupiter. The combination of flexible, precision machines and versatile, highly skilled workmen enabled a huge reduction in product development times. Multiple resources could be deployed at each stage so that bottlenecks could be prevented. The same resources — machines and people — could be used in multiple steps, thereby transferring knowledge between the steps and reducing the 'handover' problems between stages in typical product development processes. This was a strategic advantage provided by the company's human resources strategy, in those years when significant applications of computer-aided design and development had not been developed yet.

TELCO dominated the market in India for the commercial vehicles it had thus far been licensed to produce, that is, with a capacity of 8 tonnes and above. Other Indian companies had been licensed to produce vehicles below 8 tonnes. These companies had not invested in the improvement of their products. Therefore, there was a need in the country for better light commercial vehicles and the government had permitted the new Japanese joint ventures to assemble them with CKD packs imported from Japan and sell them in India. The Japanese companies introduced 6-tonne light commercial vehicles, which were just below the Tata range, and for which they expected high demand in India.

TELCO decided to 'encircle' its Japanese competitors by introducing an even lighter, 4-tonne vehicle, though it would be more difficult for the company because there would be much less commonality of parts with its existing range. In fact, a 4-tonne vehicle would require a new engine, new transmission, new brakes, and a new cabin, and many other new components. The 'encircle' strategy had been deployed by Komatsu, the Japanese earth-moving equipment producer in the 1970s to take on its much larger competitor, Caterpillar. With its 'Encircle C' strategy Komatsu had eaten into Caterpillar's markets in many countries. If TELCO had good 4-tonne and 8-tonne products in the market at the same time, the Japanese 6-tonne products would be squeezed in between.

An audacious goal, with very high levels of cooperation within the team, enabled TELCO to produce a very successful 4-tonne commercial vehicle, the Tata 407, within eighteen months. This was a world record in new product development time. Moreover, the Tata 407 was better suited to Indian conditions than Japanese products. The Japanese and their

Indian partners did not expect this to hit to them. Soon they dwindled out of the market.

Many years later, when I was consulting to automobile companies in the US, the editor of an international business magazine, who was writing a story on the US auto companies' largely unsuccessful attempts to contend with the onslaught of Japanese light trucks and cars said that the story he had really wanted to write was how an Indian company had beaten back Japanese automobile competitors many years ago.

In 1989, I had to request for a sabbatical from Tatas to live in the US for a while for family health reasons. In those days, Indian government regulations forbade directors of public limited companies to earn more than a secretary of the Government of India. I did not have any savings, and, in any case, government regulations would have prevented me from taking out any money. I had to find some way to earn and support the family in the US. Fortunately, I was hired as a senior consultant by Arthur D. Little Inc. (ADL), the world's oldest consulting company.

ADL was over a hundred years old when I reported for work at its headquarters in Cambridge, Massachusetts in April 1989. ADL was promoted by MIT (the Massachusetts Institute of Technology) to translate scientific developments into industrial applications. On the day I reported for work, I was told researchers from ADL were at work with clients in every continent—even in Antarctica, where an ADL consulting scientist was aboard the US government's research ship. Above all that, the largest number of experimental devices from any non-government organization on NASA's (National Aeronautics and Space Administration) lunar exploration vehicle, then on the moon, were ADL experimental devices. NASA was a client of ADL, as was the US Department of Defence, and many commercial organizations for whom ADL had established research laboratories.

NASA was also consulting with another, much smaller consulting company — Innovation Associates, which had been founded by Charlie Kieffer and Peter M. Senge (author of *The Fifth Discipline: The Art and Practice of the Learning Organization*[*]), both of whom were physicists from MIT. Innovation Associates, as its name suggests, specialized in assisting clients to break out of rigidities and become innovative organizations. Senge, Kieffer, and their partners in Innovation Associates specialized in the organizational and human sides of change and innovation, whereas ADL was well known for its prowess in the technological side of innovation. NASA proposed that ADL and Innovation Associates should combine their skills to consult with NASA. ADL acquired Innovation Associates and I was made the managing director of Innovation Associates with the mission to combine the best of both.

I learned about the many facets of innovation from the best of the best. Innovation has become an overused word today. It is also poorly understood. Innovation has become closely associated with technology, and 'technology' has become associated almost entirely, in the public imagination, with information, computation, and communication technologies. Technologies derived from the material sciences have been pushed into the background. Moreover, innovation has become conflated with patents. In this world of innovation, which is narrowly restricted to technologies and patents, innovations in processes and forms of institutions are forgotten, though it is innovations in processes and institutional architectures that produce the greatest benefits. The Toyota Production System that enabled just-in-time production and zero defects hardly required any new technologies. Nor was it patented. Nor

---

[*]Peter M. Senge. *The Fifth Discipline: The Art and Practice of the Learning Organization.* Crown Business, 2010.

were the systems for democratic decision-making that have advanced human well-being greatly, patentable or patented. No new technology was required.

The breakthrough performance of Project Jupiter was a result of several innovations in the design of human resource development systems, and in the design of the product development process. There were no new patents acquired nor required.

These ideas would become important during my time at the Planning Commission as well. Soon after I joined the Commission, a National Innovation Council was promoted by the Planning Commission with Dr Sam Pitroda as its chairman. I was a member. Our mission was to create an ecosystem for innovations in India that would improve the lives of the poorest people. We realized that, broadly speaking, there seemed to be two paradigms of innovation. One is 'Silicon Valley and patents innovation'. In this paradigm, lots of money must be invested in formal 'R&D', many scientists must be engaged, and many patents must be produced. The other is 'frugal innovation', which does not require money to create the innovations, and which produces affordable solutions for people with very small incomes. In the first paradigm, the purpose of innovation is to make money for inventors and investors. In the second paradigm, the purpose of innovation is to find affordable solutions to improve the lives of people.

Innovation does not require much money. In fact, too much money reduces the pressure to be innovative. When I joined ADL in 1989, automobile industry analysts were predicting which automobile companies would survive global competition. Their hypothesis was that companies would need to invest lots of money in R&D and in new product development to win. They compared the R&D budgets and financial resources for product development of all companies. Their conclusion was that General Motors, who had the largest budgets, would surely be a winner, and the small Honda Motor Company would not survive. My colleagues in ADL and I had the opposite view. We believed that those companies that had the greatest drive to win and the least money would be the most innovative and would win. Our bet was that Honda would be a winner and that General Motors would throw large amounts of money at problems and yet not win. We were right.

Japanese companies did not have the resources in the 1970s and 1980s that their much larger American and European competitors had. They were determined to win. They concentrated on innovations in processes to get more from less. They excelled in involving shop-floor workers and junior engineers in the improvement of enterprise performance.

These same Japanese ways were the ways in which the managers of Tatab and the managers and employees of TELCO were able to win—even over the Japanese themselves.

NINE

CRISES OF ASPIRATION

Any team that learns to work together much better than others can will win even if it has less resources. Both the Tatab team and the Project Jupiter team proved this. Both also proved that Indians can do amazing things when they work together more effectively, including beating the world's best.

For Tatab in Malaysia there was a 'crisis of condition' — monetary losses and an ultimatum from the bank to close the company. In Project Jupiter there was no crisis of condition. Tatas were doing well — there was no immediate prospect of Tatas, the largest company in the industry, making a loss. In both situations the team overcame 'a painful discrepancy' in the strength and knowledge it had by setting an aspirational goal for itself that every member became emotionally connected with. The quality of the 'inner game' is the key to success in the 'outer game', especially when the goal seems impossible.

The inner game is driven by a crisis of aspiration — a challenge created for oneself, not a target imposed by others. The target to make Tatab profitable in three years was set by the bank. The aspiration to prove that Indians were equal to the best came from within and was a self-driven aspiration. As Alexander said, 'The gods put dreams and aspirations into the hearts of men....' He did not *need* to go to India; he deeply wanted to. Still the chatter around you and ask yourself the question, what do you care for most of all? You may evoke your deep aspiration, your cause, for which you will do much more than you might for the goal imposed on you by others.

Personal circumstances with the health and education of my children took me away from Tatas and India for ten years to the US, where I had to find a way to earn to support my family. As mentioned earlier, I joined a consulting company to advise clients in the US to improve their manufacturing capabilities to beat foreign competition, principally from Japan. I was hired by a Mexican company which feared an existential crisis when Mexico signed the North American Free Trade Agreement (NAFTA) with the US and Canada, which would give easy entry to large US corporations into the Mexican market, which the Mexican company had dominated hitherto.

In every case where manufacturing performance must improve, I would examine the corporate strategy and I would 'rub my nose on the company's shop-floor', an expression that Mr Moolgaokar had taught me when he posted me to the Tata factory in Pune. I would attend the night shifts in auto parts factories in Detroit and Pittsburgh, when mostly black workers would be at work. I went to factories of the Mexican company in remote parts of the country and, with the help of my Spanish-speaking colleagues, listened to the concerns and personal aspirations of the workers and to their suggestions for improving the performance of their factories.

Always I noticed an untapped potential in the companies, in the power of their human assets — their employees — to learn and improve their own capabilities, and with that to improve the competitiveness and performance of their companies' factories. In the conventional strategic view, the employees were a cost to be minimized, especially when financial conditions were tough. In actuality, the employees could be the source of the new competitive energy the company needed to turn around the company's performance. They are the only 'appreciating assets' any company has. Human beings can learn and improve their own capabilities over time if they are motivated and enabled to: all other assets of a factory — its machines, its buildings, its materials — will inevitably depreciate in value. Human beings drive themselves with 'crises of aspiration' which machines, materials, and buildings cannot have.

The only source of sustainable competitive advantage for a company is its ability to learn, change, and improve faster than any potential competition. In a globalized world where new competitors can appear from other countries, a world in which boundaries of industries are also being blurred by new technologies and new business models, competition can come from players in other industries too.

In this dynamically changing and uncertain world, one cannot be certain where competition will come from next and who the competition will be. Therefore, companies must be able to change fast, and to change fast they must learn fast. The pace at which a company's sales and its profits grow is ultimately determined by the pace at which the company learns and changes. For this it must recognize that its people are its only appreciating assets: they are the key to the pace at which a company can learn, innovate, and change. My colleagues in consulting urged me to write about my experience and insights. I wrote two books: *The Accelerating Organization: Embracing the Face of Human Change* (published by McGraw Hill International in 1996), and *Shaping the Future: Aspirational Leadership in India and Beyond* (published by John Wiley and Sons in 2002), and then a third: *Remaking India: One Country, One Destiny* (published by Response Books in 2004). All this while I was consulting to companies and business associations, many abroad and many in India.

Through my journeys in India, Malaysia, North America, South America, and Europe, working with teams who produced remarkable results, sometimes as the leader of the team, sometimes as a member, and sometimes as a consultant, I learned the power of a shared aspirational vision. When a group of people come together, and set for themselves a goal which fulfils their deep aspirations, they create an essential condition for converting a bunch of competent individuals into a high-performing team. This aspirational vision aligns them and encourages them to support each other, because each will fulfil his or her aspiration only when the others do too.

Very often I have used a slide to make this important point because a picture can say more than words. When I joined the Planning Commission, the cabinet secretary of the Indian government requested me to run workshops for senior civil servants to introduce them to methods for strategic change. I was also invited to teach these ideas at the civil services' training academy in Mussoorie. I found that Indian civil servants care greatly for the condition of the country, and that they are generally frustrated by the conditions within government—the internal silos and the mindless procedures. They wonder how more cooperation can be created within government, which will benefit the country greatly—and which they would enjoy too. I would often use some slides in these workshops: indeed, it seemed to be expected of me, as a former consultant, to make a power-point presentation! The one slide that many participants in these workshops said they found most powerful was this slide of the magnet. Here I present this slide which illustrates the power of a shared aspirational vision.

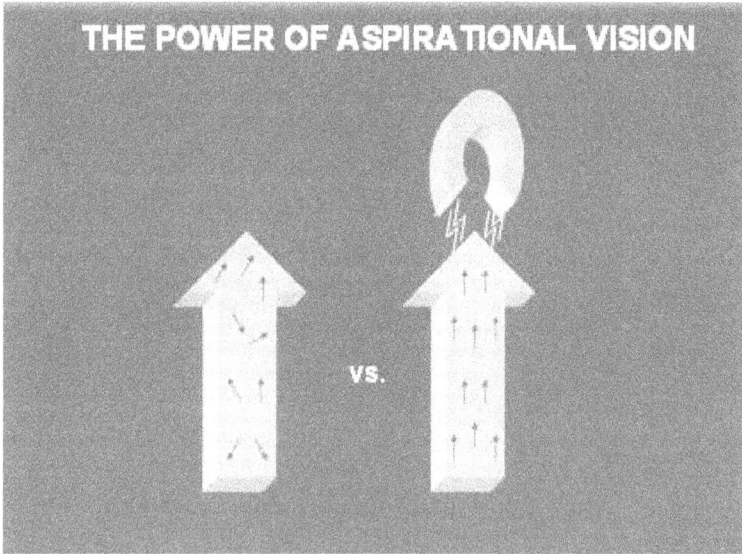

Figure 1: From contention to collaboration.

Part Two

Shaping Our Future

◆

The future has to be lived before it can be written about.

Jawaharlal Nehru,

An Autobiography, with Musings on Recent Events in India[*]

Nothing is more difficult to take in hand, more perilous to conduct or more uncertain of success, than to take the lead in the introduction of a new order of things.

Niccolo Machiavelli, *The Prince*[**]

*Jawaharlal Nehru. *An Autobiography, with Musings on Recent Events in India.* Allied Publishers, 1962.
**Niccolo Machiavelli (trans. Daniel Donno). *The Prince.* Open Road Media, 2014.

ONE

MY GRANDSON'S ADVICE

A child's honest observation is often a sharp wake-up call, as was a child's observation in the fable of the Emperor's new clothes that the Emperor, strutting proudly before his people, was actually naked.

My grandson, Viren, who lives with his parents in the US, visited us in India in 2008, when he was five years old. I had not yet joined the Planning Commission.

I took him with his parents for a drive to see the sights of New Delhi. I was driving, with my son beside me and Viren and his mother in the back-seat. We had stopped at a traffic light on Lodhi Road. When it turned green, and I moved on, I heard him say, 'Mom, you did not answer the lady who was knocking on the window!' She asked, 'Which lady, Viren?' He said, 'The lady with the baby in her arms who was knocking on the window when we had stopped.' She said, 'I am sorry, Viren, I was pre-occupied and did not notice her.'

Then he asked, 'Mom, why do they have to do everything on the street?' She asked, 'Do what, Viren?' He replied, 'Everything. They were sleeping on the side of the street. They were cooking there. And, Mom, I think I saw a little girl doing poo-poo too.' She said, 'Viren, they are very poor. There are lots of poor people in India. They do not have money to live in a house with bedrooms, a kitchen, and bathrooms, which richer people like us have.'

Two years later, when he was seven, his family visited us again. I had been in the Planning Commission for a year then. We drove along Lodhi Road once again. Viren was very silent. When we turned at the corner past the Nizamuddin village, Viren exploded. 'What is the government doing? Counting daisies!'

His father asked him, 'Counting daisies? What do you mean?' Viren replied, 'There are so many poor people. Does the government know? Why is the government not doing anything for them?' It was a surprising observation because the Planning Commission was engaged in a public debate then about how many poor people there were in India and where the poverty line should be drawn. His father said, 'Viren, pipe down! Dadaji, your grandfather, is in the government now. He is in the Planning Commission.'

When we got home, Viren asked me what the Planning Commission was. I showed him the volumes of the Eleventh Five Year Plan, copies of which I had at home. He did not seem impressed. I took him with me to Yojana Bhavan to my office the next day. He was very impressed with the numbers of cars with red lights he saw in the courtyard, and with the size of my room, and with my official door-opener who smiled and returned Viren's salute (unlike the policemen who seemed oblivious to the car with the red beacon when we drove past them).

When Viren returned to his school after his summer holiday in India, his class had to write an account of what they had done in the holidays. Viren wrote a book on India's Planning Commission, with a contents page, chapters, illustrations, and a glossary of terms too! It is an illustrated book with pictures that Viren has drawn. I reproduce two pages of the book here with Viren's permission. He refers to the Planning Commission as the Planning Community, suggesting sub-consciously how he thinks planning should work with the participation of the people. He also has great expectations of the Planning Commission (or Community). He says it will bring about a big change in the lives of poor people.

In the evening, after we had visited the Planning Commission's office in Yojana Bhavan, I had asked Viren what his impressions had been. He was bouncing a ball. He tapped it a few more times, then paused, ball in hand. 'Dadaji, don't write more of those fat books,' he said, pointing to the Eleventh Plan volumes on the shelf. 'Do something!'

The prime minister had asked me to do something to improve the Planning Commission, a sixty-year-old institution. What should be done and how?

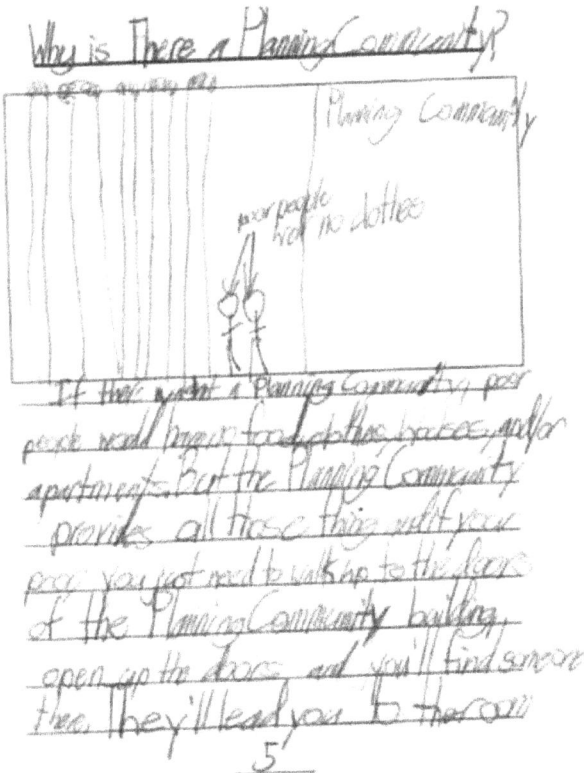

Why is There a Planning Community?

Planning Community

poor people had no clothes

If there wasn't a Planning Community poor people would have no food, clothes, houses and/or apartments. But the Planning Community provides all those things. If you're poor you just need to walk up to the floor of the Planning Community building, open up the door and you'll find someone there. They'll lead you to the room.

5

(i)

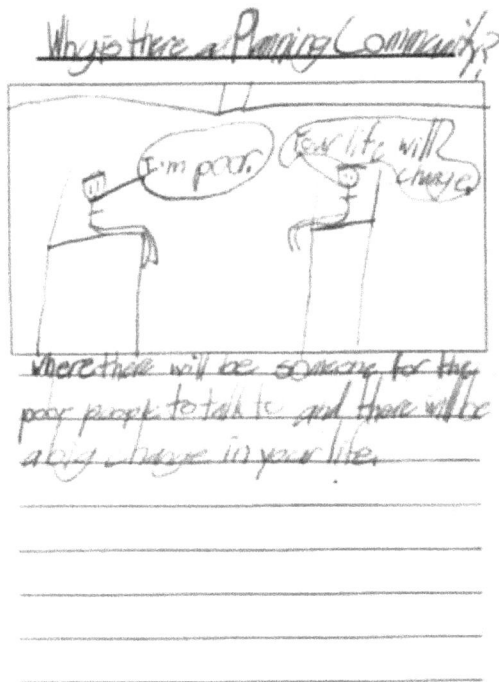

(ii)

Figure 2 (i and ii): The purpose of the
Planning Commission according to Viren.

TWO

CHANGE IT IF YOU CAN

The question Dr Manmohan Singh posed to me in 2009 after I joined the Planning Commission was what could be done to reform the Planning Commission, which had resisted many attempts to make significant changes to it.

I suggested that the first question one should ask is this: if India did not have a Planning Commission in 2009, would one set up an institution for planning now? And if so, what purpose would one expect this institution to serve for India's development? And what functions should it perform?

I recommended that these questions should be put to leaders of industry, civil society, and government. They should be asked what sort of planning institution the country would need now, if any, to accelerate its overall development in twenty-first century conditions, which are different from the conditions in which the Commission had been set up soon after the country's independence. Accordingly, I was given a list of twenty leaders from diverse fields who would have good insights into the country's requirements.

They were very happy to meet me and generously gave me their candid views. I asked each of these leaders three questions:

1. Is the Planning Commission playing a useful role for the country?

2. If not, is there another role that the Planning Commission should play in the country's progress?
3. In what way could the Commission transform itself to play this role?

The answer to the first question was unanimous. The Planning Commission was no longer making a significant contribution to the progress of the country. The country had changed. It had become more decentralized, both politically and economically, since the Planning Commission was set up in the 1950s. The private sector was playing an increasingly larger role now, and the Indian economy was more connected with the international economy. For all these reasons, the Five Year Plans, made by some experts in Delhi still following the top-down Soviet planning model, which had to be implemented by people across the country, were not very useful.

However, everyone, including the industrialists, said that the dynamic nature of the changes in India and outside required that there be a strategic group that could sense the forces that were causing change to happen and that would provide governments in the centre and in the states, and private industry too, with insights into the forces shaping the future. These thought leaders wanted the Planning Commission to lift itself out of the rut of allocating funds and approving proposals and play a more strategic role in shaping the country's future.

Ratan Tata, then the chairman of the Tata group, is a pilot too. He used the metaphor of a radar to suggest what the role of the Planning Commission could be when there are many private enterprises, each with their own boards of management, and many states with governments from different political parties, who must chart their own courses. All the pilots voluntarily take guidance from a radar, which suggests to them the best course they may take for a safe journey for all the passengers aboard for whose lives they are accountable. To provide this service, the Planning Commission will have to learn modern methods of planning, such as scenario planning.

Another leader, who had retired from the government, having held many senior positions, including that of Governor of the Reserve Bank, said the country needed an institution to create a 'glue' to bond separate entities, and not a 'boss' over them. Coordination amongst independent institutions was required, such as the state governments, the private sector, and regulators. However, they could not be — indeed must not be — coordinated through command-and-control, or they would lose their independence. Processes for lateral coordination had become necessary. Could a reformed Planning Commission provide the glue?

The Planning Commission was formed soon after India's Independence to enable the development of the country and improve the welfare of all its citizens equitably. The government's resources were very scarce then, and the gaps to be filled were very large. Therefore the allocation of resources had to be a principal function of the Planning Commission.

India was not the only country at that time that had a large need to build or rebuild public infrastructure and improve or restore living conditions of people, with the concomitant need to ensure that resources were deployed well. After the Second World War, many countries had such problems, including Japan, Germany, France, Korea, China, the Soviet Union, and, to a lesser extent, even the US. In all these countries, their governments set up processes to direct scarce resources towards the country's priorities. Planning was necessary, and planning was done in most countries with very good results. There were quicker results in some cases, such as Japan, Germany, and France, where there were pre-existing institutional infrastructures for managing the economy. Dramatic results came later in other countries, such as Korea and China, who, along with the planning and allocation of resources, had to also build other institutional abilities.

The Soviet Union had adopted formal planning for development before many of these countries. It was a noteworthy example of a country that had been able to lift the standard of living of millions of people and to introduce equity into a very iniquitous society. If planning was required, then the Soviet model of planning would seem to be an attractive one to follow for a developing country with the ambitions India had. The toxic side-effects of the overly controlling Soviet model of planning became evident in the Soviet Union (and in India) much later.

It was not the idea of planning that was the problem, it was the method of planning that turned out to be wrong. In fact, Milton Friedman, the economist most often associated with the idea that the best way to grow an economy is to let market forces reign, said in 1963, after a visit to India, that he was not against planning but against the type of bad planning practised by India's Planning Commission following the Soviet model.

Other countries that have effectively used formal planning methods to grow their economies, some remarkable examples being South Korea and China, modified their planning processes with changing conditions—changing internal conditions such as the shape of their economies as they developed, as well as changes in the external environment. On the other hand, India's planning process carried on, barely reformed. The title of a book by the economist Dr Vivek Chibber, which contrasts the histories of planning in Korea and India, both of which set up similar planning processes at about the same time, is telling. Its title is *Locked in Place*[*]:

---

[*]Dr Vivek Chibber. *Locked in Place: State-Building and Late Industrialization in India.* Princeton University Press, 2006.

an evocative description of the planning institutions of India.

The Planning Commission of India, locked into an outmoded and increasingly less useful mode of planning, was becoming less and less effective to fulfil the purpose it was expected to achieve in the country's economy. According to many knowledgable observers, it was mostly serving the purposes of its own members and staff. They said it had become a 'parking lot' for bureaucrats between postings, and others who could not be placed anywhere else. It also provided a pedestal to place unsuccessful politicians and friends of the powerful. Their visibility to the public from this pedestal would satisfy their egos. For such people, the Planning Commission was an institution for their personal convenience and a pedestal to use. In their minds, they did not have a responsibility to improve its condition. Perhaps the condition of the Planning Commission had deteriorated too much with poor leadership for too long.

The Government Resolution of 15 March 1950 setting up the Planning Commission said, 'Its success will depend on the extent to which it enlists the association and cooperation of the people at all levels.' If the people of the country and the politicians they elect have to support the plans, and also play a role in their implementation, then it is necessary that they should understand the plans. However, very few, even amongst these leaders of the country that I interviewed, had read the Five Year Plans. The documents were too long, running up to a thousand pages, much of them written in economists' jargon, and with numbers that often did not appear connected with the realities of people's lives. If these highly educated citizens had found the plans inaccessible, imagine what the common woman and man could find in them!

Dr Manmohan Singh met the Planning Commission, of which he was the chairman, only once or twice a year. The meetings were short, never more than an hour and half, and very formal. The Members were seated in their order of seniority, which was the date on which they had joined the Commission. Each was expected to speak for six or seven minutes in turn though some would take longer. The prime minister would ask some questions directly to the Members, though not often. Having heard all, the prime minister would make brief concluding observations. I had been the last to join because I had to re-acquire my Indian citizenship (and give up the American citizenship I had acquired when I was living in the US), which had taken some time. Therefore, I was the last to speak—and in some meetings never got a chance because the time had run out!

What the mirror on the wall had said to the Planning Commission, in the voices of the eminent citizens I had consulted, was reported by the deputy chairman and members of the Planning Commission to the prime minister in April 2010. In this meeting, the prime minister, who is an excellent listener, though a reluctant speaker, was very interested in what I had to report. He referred to me as 'the change management expert'.

Dr Manmohan Singh heard the report. Then he gave directions for the reform of the Planning Commission. He said that the Planning Commission must become a 'Systems Reform Commission' rather than a budget-making body. And that the Planning Commission must become 'an essay (that is a force) in persuasion', rather than a writer of long plans.

THREE

A STRATEGY FOR CHANGE

I have consulted with organizations in the private, non-government, and government sectors in many countries on strategies for change, so the voice (along with the jargon) of consultants may come easily to me. I will now put on my consultant hat—and speak in the voice of a 'change management expert', as Dr Manmohan Singh kindly described me.

Often, before I begin a discussion with the leadership team of an organization on strategies to get the best performance from their organizations, I ask each of them to take a piece of paper and draw a sketch of 'an institution'. Invariably, the majority will draw an organization chart with a hierarchy of positions. Some will make a picture of a building or a factory. But some, most often women in the group, will draw sketches of people, or a network (rather than a hierarchy) with intersecting relationships. Rarely, some will also write words, such as 'values' and 'behaviours'.

Institutions are not concrete edifices. Nor can they be described by organizational charts. The norms and ideas that guide people and the ways in which they conduct their affairs are integral to institutions. For example, the 'institution' of parliamentary democracy in Britain has evolved over many centuries. The core of an institution is the ways in which decisions are taken and discussions are conducted. Institutions may require spaces and buildings to perform some of their functions, such as the magnificent buildings in Westminster along the Thames in London in which the members of Britain's Parliament meet, and where the staff who support them have their offices. But one cannot understand what parliamentary democracy is and what purpose it serves in the lives of Britain's citizens merely from the size and shape of the Parliament's buildings and from the numbers of staff within them and their titles.

Institutions have 'structures', but institutions function through 'processes'. Some structures of an institution are its name, its internal organizational arrangements, with its hierarchy and staffing, and the place and buildings from which its staff operate. When asked 'What is this institution, and where is it', this is the information that is usually provided. Such features of an institution—its name, the shape and size of its buildings, their location, even the organizational chart—can be described in 'concrete' terms. However, as in the example of the British Parliament mentioned before, such easily accessible 'concrete' information cannot explain the purpose of the institution and how it functions.

Institutions function through processes with which they deliver value for their stakeholders. Therefore, to increase the value that an institution provides its stakeholders, its processes must be improved. Small changes in processes by modifying some procedures may be sufficient if the improvements required are not large. In many cases, however, a more substantial re-engineering of processes is required: for example, to take advantage of new computation and communication technologies. Indeed, it was the advent of digital information technologies in the 1990s which brought about a wave of 'process re-engineering' projects in the corporate sector, which subsequently extended to the public sector, where it continues in many 'e-governance' projects.

Noting the views of the leaders who were consulted and the needs of the country in the twenty-first century, the prime minister directed that the Planning Commission must change from being a fund allocating body to become a provider of radar signals to pilots. For this, it would have to adopt new processes and dispense with old ones. For example, re-engineering processes for funds allocation to improve their efficiency would not be sufficient reform. New processes for looking into the future would have to be introduced.

Concrete structures are not the institution. However, an institution's structures enable the institution to perform processes. When these structures are aligned with the requirements of the processes, they improve the institution's effectiveness. When they are misaligned, they become hindrances. Think of this analogy: when the purpose of a building has to be changed from being a residence to becoming an office, the locations of interior walls, and sizes and shapes of rooms, can create restrictions on what an architect can do. It may be possible to overcome some of the restrictions by pulling down some walls. But some resistances to change, like the load-bearing walls of the building, are more embedded and less changeable, and the architect must work around them.

With this reflection on the substance of institutions, I return to the institution of the Indian Planning Commission.

The processes within the Indian Planning Commission are integrally linked to the wider processes of the Indian government. The Planning Commission could not unilaterally stop doing its old work and begin doing something else instead, even if its own reform may require this. For example, the Planning Commission could not unilaterally stop allocating funds and approving ministries' budget proposals, to convert itself from a finance allocating body into a Systems Reform Commission as the prime minister had directed. The work of government would stop. The files would not know where to go! Therefore, a broader reform of government processes would be required and the finance allocating and budget approval processes would have to be assigned elsewhere.

The reform of the Planning Commission would require radically new ways of planning and new ways of interacting with the states and other stakeholders. Radically new processes often require people with different mind-sets to conduct them. People in entrenched ways of thinking and working will resist the adoption of radically different processes. It was not possible to change the people in the Planning Commission because its staffing systems were embedded in the large mesh of personnel systems of the government. Staff came into the Planning Commission from government cadres—the Indian Economics Service, the Indian Statistical Service, and the Indian Administrative Service (IAS). The career management of these staff—their transfers, postings, and training—was managed by people outside the Planning Commission who were disconnected from its needs.

Often one cannot change the people in an organization. However, one can try to change the way they work. One of the very first steps, after the meeting with the prime minister where he had directed the change of the Planning Commission, was a meeting of all the officers of the Planning Commission to explain to them why the processes of the Planning Commission had to be reformed, and what the processes had to be reformed to do.

Montek did not come to the meeting. He asked me to explain the case for change to the officers. He felt they would be more candid if he was not present. There were over fifty officers in the meeting. A few were enthusiastic that change must be brought about, but a few were cynical, even hostile. To understand an institution, one has to work in it for a long time, they said. One should not rely on the views of outsiders, as most of the people I had interviewed were, they said. (And as I was too, they seemed to imply!) The majority listened keenly and did not speak. It was the typical Bell curve distribution encountered in any change programme: 10 per cent to 20 per cent enthusiasts who will lead the change; 10 per cent to 20 per cent cynics who may never change; and the remaining 60 per cent to 80 per cent who will wait to see which way the tide goes.

The next morning some junior staff came to see me. They had heard about the meeting with the officers the previous day. They asked me to meet with the junior staff too. They were very interested in how the Planning Commission could be improved. So there was another large meeting the next day. I asked for a round of introductions, and requested each person to say how long they had worked in the Planning Commission. Many had worked a long time; some even more than thirty years. They said this was the first time in their memory that a member of the Planning Commission had talked to the junior staff so candidly about the purpose of the Planning Commission and how it could serve the country better.

Over the next few days, several senior officers came to see me individually. They told me how pleased they were that a radical reform was being considered of the way the Planning Commission was functioning. They said they wanted to serve the country — which is why they were in government. And some said: I do not earn much in government, nor do I want to make more money. My life is passing by. I want to do some good for the country. They knew they were not doing enough, they said. There was too much pettiness, too many turf battles, and too little learning within the Planning Commission to provide the value to the country that it should provide. They assured their support for the changes required if they were involved.

Attempts had been made before to change the decision-criteria of the civil services to fit the Planning Commission's needs. They had failed. When I was asked by Montek and the prime minister to apply my knowledge of change management to improving the Planning Commission, I decided to ask what those who had tried to change the Planning Commission before had learned, so that we would not repeat any mistakes. The most recent effort to reform the Planning Commission had been made during the era of the previous National Democratic Alliance (NDA) government, between 2000 and 2004. I was able to interview several people who had been involved with that effort. One of them was a lady officer in the Commission who had been a leader of an internal team that had been set up to support the external consultants who had been engaged for the reform. I met the consultants also, who were very candid in their reflections. I also discussed what lessons were learned with Dr N.C. Saxena, who was the Secretary of the Planning Commission when the reform had been attempted.

The lady officer was amongst the 10 per cent of passionate enthusiasts for the reform of the Planning Commission. She was due to retire soon. She said that she had great regret for how little the Planning Commission was doing to make a difference to the lives of the poorer citizens of India. There was so much to be done. She was sad too about how little she had been able to do. She prayed that the Planning Commission would reform itself to have a greater impact on the livelihoods of the poorest people in the country. She said that many staff of the Planning Commission, including herself, had participated very enthusiastically in the previous effort to reform the Planning Commission. They were disappointed when there was no change. Even though she would not be around, since she would retire, she prayed that the reform process would succeed this time. She introduced the consultants to me.

The consultants were generous: they gave me their reports. And they were very candid. They had failed to have an impact because they spent their time and energy doing the wrong things. They had described a new organizational structure for the Planning Commission and had written detailed job descriptions for the principal positions in it. Those changes were never made and, as the consultants admitted, could not have been made, because the top leadership of the Planning Commission—the deputy chairman and the chairman (the prime minister)—was not involved in the exercise. Structural changes are always difficult to implement because people's jobs, and positions of power, are affected. Therefore, they can be made only by the top leadership. Its 'political will' is required to effect the changes. When the top leadership is not involved with the reform exercise, or only gives it half-hearted support, structural change should not be the strategy for reform, they advised.

Dr N.C. Saxena confirmed the consultants' analysis. He said that a structural reform of the Planning Commission was required but it was very difficult. It would involve changes in many staffing systems of the government outside the purview of the Planning Commission itself. For example, the cabinet secretary (and prime minister) must not 'park' senior IAS officers in the Planning Commission. And the quality of staff from the Indian Economic Service, which was a prime source for officers for the Planning Commission, would have to be improved. However, the Planning Commission did not run the service: it was managed principally by the economic adviser to the finance minister. Thus the reform of the Planning Commission's structure and its staffing were pieces of a much broader re-structuring of the administrative services which was also overdue.

I interviewed two former cabinet secretaries for advice on how to approach the reform of the Planning Commission. Both confirmed what Dr Saxena had said. The Planning Commission was a 'holding place' (the term they preferred more than 'parking lot') for IAS officers. Running a large government was complicated. Many contingencies had to be provided for, they suggested. 'If highways did not have strategically placed lay-bys on their sides, where tired drivers or crippled vehicles could temporarily park, the flow of traffic on the highway would be impeded,' one of them pointed out. They did not deny that the Planning Commission had staffing problems. But their own priorities were other functions of the government, not the Planning Commission.

Since the Planning Commission was embedded in a larger government system, Dr Saxena confirmed that major reforms of the Planning Commission must have the weight of the prime minister behind them and the unwavering commitment of the deputy chairman. Since, this time, it seemed that the prime minister himself and the deputy chairman of the Planning Commission were sponsoring the change, perhaps it would happen now, he hoped. He wished me good luck.

Indeed, there was widespread expectation that the time the Planning Commission would be reformed had come at last. A senior journalist, who had been writing about the process of economic reforms in the country and about the Planning Commission for many years, came to interview me when Montek announced to the media that the Planning Commission would be reformed and that I would play a role in the process. The journalist said that the stars were in the right configuration for the reform of the Planning Commission. Dr Manmohan Singh and Montek Ahluwalia had been credited with the leadership of the economic reforms in the early 1990s. They had opened up the economy to private enterprise and to foreign competition by dismantling systems of economic planning and control that had been choking economic growth. The reform of the Planning Commission was unfinished business. Dr Manmohan Singh had returned triumphantly as prime minister of India in 2009. Montek was re-appointed the deputy chairman of the Planning Commission. Both had five years of experience behind them as the chairman and the deputy chairman of the Planning Commission. They knew what the difficulties of reforming it were. Their political stock was very high in 2009. They were the best team to lead the reform of the Planning Commission. In his opinion, there could not be a better time to reform the Planning Commission. This was also the view of many other people both inside and outside it.

I had been involved with many institutional change programmes, and I had researched methods and written about them. I knew that even when the leadership team was committed, and the need to change had been acknowledged, one should never underestimate the resistance that will arise to changes in organizational structures and staffing patterns. The resistance to change comes from within, and often there is opposition from vested interests outside the organization. Opposition to changes in the Planning Commission had stalled all previous attempts to reform it. Perhaps even Dr Manmohan Singh's and Montek's will and their political skills to make the change would not be enough. Wisdom said that it would be best not to bang one's head again against the walls of opposition again. It would be wiser to adopt another strategy. If the Planning Commission's structures – analogous to a computer's hardware – seemed unalterable, perhaps new software could be applied to change its performance.

The strategy for change would be to create a 'Plus' to the Planning Commission with new processes rather than attempt to alter its rigid organizational structure. The 'Plus' would be new processes for the Planning Commission to become an 'essay in persuasion' and a 'Systems Reform Commission'. These processes could be developed by those members of the Planning Commission who were committed to bring about the reforms, by leveraging resources outside the Planning Commission, and engaging some motivated officers within it.

FOUR

CONNECTING THE DOTS

The Planning Commission's 'flagship product' was the Five Year Plan. It had made eleven of these since its inception in 1950 and it was time to prepare the twelfth. Because the Commission's rigid structures could not be altered, a decision was taken to adopt a new process to prepare the Twelfth Five Year Plan, and thus begin to reform the Commission with a process 'Plus'. The process the Planning Commission had used in the past to prepare a Five Year Plan was for its Members and internal divisions to set up consultations for the subjects they were assigned in the organization structure. They would also prepare drafts of their chapters of the plan. A certain number of pages would be allocated to each chapter so that the entire plan document did not exceed a pre-determined length of 800 to 1000 pages.

This legacy process placed great limitations on producing any out-of-box, systemic solutions. It was 'boxed-in' in many ways. To begin with, the divisions operated within their silos. There was hardly any significant consultation across the division's boundaries. The practice was for files to move from an office in one division to an office in another division: even when their offices were side-by-side. It was unusual for people to walk across and debate with others across a table. Thus, the walls in between people were of both concrete and organizational kinds.

Moreover, the subjects assigned to the divisions were pre-determined by the subjects historically allocated to them in the organizational chart. If a new subject, which had become important to consider for the country's progress, had to be addressed in the plan, it was not clear how it would be addressed and by whom. For example, 'innovation' and 'governance' had become very important for India when the Twelfth Plan was being formulated. But there was no division that had been officially assigned these subjects and therefore, they became difficult to consider while formulating the plan.

Finally, the format of the plan barely changed. The format, style, and length of the previous plan were used as guides while preparing the next one. In fact, many critics said that each Five Year Plan seemed the same as the previous one, only with a few numbers changed!

The ailments of the Planning Commission's organization (and the government's too) can be described in words from Rabindranath Tagore's poem, *Gitanjali**. He describes a heaven of freedom in which 'the world has not been broken into fragments by narrow domestic walls', and in which 'the clear stream of reason has not lost its way in the dreary desert sand of dead habit.' Freedom seemed to have been lost within the Commission due to its walls and its dreary habits.

The Government of India decided to introduce a system for the performance management of the ministries in 2008. Dr Prajapati Trivedi took leave from the Kennedy School of Public Policy at Harvard University to take on the assignment full-time in India. Detailed formats were developed in which the ministries would, every year, state the goals they would achieve in the next year. Then, at the end of the year, their achievements would be evaluated. In the first year, questions were raised about this process, which was known as the RFD

---

*Rabindranath Tagore. *Gitanjali*. General Book Depot, 2009.

(Results Framework Document) process. Since the expectation was that the performance of ministries may be evaluated quite seriously, and since there was also some talk about linking the compensation of senior bureaucrats with such evaluations, the ministries were playing safe. They mentioned goals which were easy to measure (and easy to achieve) and which were within their own ministry's control. To choose a goal for the achievement of which other ministries' collaboration was required was risky. What if the other ministry did not collaborate and perform? Moreover, how would credit be assigned for such collaborative work?

Most of the big issues the country faces require collaboration between many ministries. For example, children's welfare, even though it has a department dedicated to it in the Ministry of Women and Child Development, requires improvements in health systems and education systems for which there are other large and powerful ministries. Improvement of health requires improvement in sanitation and the availability of clean water, especially in India, which are the purviews of other ministries. Another subject of great importance to India, the development of skills that will lead to gainful employment, requires collaboration between the Ministry of Labour and Employment and the Ministry of Education on the 'supply' side of skills, and the many ministries on the 'demand' side who are responsible for the growth of enterprises, such as the Ministry of Commerce and Industry, the Ministry of Micro, Small, and Medium enterprises, the Ministry of Heavy Industry, and so on.

The cabinet secretary, who was overseeing the RFD process, and Dr Trivedi considered that the Planning Commission would have a crucial role to play. The Planning Commission could explain which ministries and departments were required to collaborate for which national goals. This would be a good starting point for the RFD exercise. The ministries and departments concerned could be asked to work out joint goals for these national objectives. However, the Planning Commission was not able to do this. It was as much divided by its internal domestic walls as was the government.

When, for example, it was becoming clear that job creation and skill development cannot be separated, the difficulty of getting the divisions within the Planning Commission itself to work together came in the way. At one stage, I asked the Advisor for Industry to meet the Advisor for Labour and Employment face-to-face, and come up with a coordinated plan. I said I would only see them together after they had met. Weeks passed. Apparently they could not agree who should go to who's room since they were at the same level. Meanwhile, they exchanged notes on file defending their narrow positions. A clear stream of reason could not find its way out of domestic walls and dead habits.

A body which was expected to be a 'Systems Reform' Commission for the country must reform its own systems also, especially when its internal systems disable it from taking a systemic view. Therefore the first step to formulate the Twelfth Plan would have to be the creation of a new internal process for connecting many dots so that the patterns in the forces shaping the country's economy and society could be seen. Dr Pronab Sen, a Principal Advisor in the Planning Commission, who had been involved in the shaping of the two previous Five Year Plans, and I were given the task of creating a process to connect the dots.

The first step was to get the officers in the Planning Commission to think outside their silos. Pronab designed a matrix of issues as a starting point. None of these issues fell completely into any division's box. They required many divisions to put their heads together, and to work in cross-divisional teams, to take a systemic view. Every officer in the Planning Commission was assigned to one or more of these teams. The teams were given a template for their work and deadlines to get it done. This process created an internal churning within the Planning Commission to break it out of embedded silos.

The output of the teams was fed into a two-day offsite meeting, organized over a weekend, at the Pusa Agriculture Institute in Delhi. Over 200 officers of the Commission came together, along with the members of the Planning Commission, to connect the outputs of their teams and to distil the systemic challenges that must be addressed for the country's progress in the next plan. Hundreds of challenges emerged. It was easy to make a laundry list of them, but a long laundry list would not be very useful. Therefore, the officers applied their minds together and distilled the list of challenges, to get to their essentials, and produced a short list of the twelve most important challenges.

These were:

1. Enhancing the capacity for growth
2. Enhancing skills and faster generation of employment
3. Managing the environment
4. Markets for efficiency and inclusion
5. Decentralization, empowerment, and information
6. Technology and innovation
7. Securing the energy future for India
8. Accelerated development of transport infrastructure
9. Rural transformation and sustained growth of agriculture
10. Managing urbanization
11. Improved access to quality education
12. Better preventive and curative healthcare

This was the first time in its recent history that the Planning Commission had organized a systematic, cross-divisional, out-of-boxes process within the Planning Commission to find the systemic challenges of the country's economy and society. The buzz within the Planning Commission was unusual. People came out of their boxes, walked around, and mingled with each other like they had not done before. The atmosphere of the offsite meeting in the Pusa Institute was full of energy and enthusiasm. Teams sent 'ambassadors' to other teams to listen to their deliberations and to invite them to join their own team's discussions. Scores of meetings between teams were scheduled in dozens of meeting rooms around the campus. People were seen carrying flip-charts across the lawns from one meeting to another. Finally, all the teams came together in a large plenary meeting where teams presented what they had learned and what their recommendations were. Then, by multi-voting, they produced the shortlist of twelve challenges.

The contrast between this energetic process of working across boundaries and the stiff formalities within the Planning Commission could not have been greater. Within the walls of Yojana Bhavan, the Planning Commission was divided into many parts. Here it was becoming one organization from many parts.

The organization and facilitation of this intense process culminating in the offsite at the Pusa Institute, which had to be completed within two months to meet the deadlines for the planning process, was enabled by a few young interns in the Planning Commission who formed themselves into a team to support Pronab Sen and me. Harsh Shrivastava led this team. Harsh, who was older than the others, had resigned a job in the private sector to work as a consultant in the Commission on a much lower salary, because he wanted to serve the country. Before he joined the private sector, he had worked in the office of the former prime minister of India, Atal Bihari Vajpayee. Having worked for a few years since then with business companies, he was yearning to work again for a larger cause and for the country.

The others in this ad hoc team were interns, mostly college students, hired by the Planning Commission to give them exposure to how the government worked and how plans were made. Each had been assigned to a division of the Planning Commission. They were permitted by their divisions to join the ad hoc team to support Harsh to manage the complex coordination of the dozens of cross-functional teams that were set up to look into the matrix of issues that Pronab Sen had made to begin the intellectual churning in the Planning Commission.

The twelve challenges that were distilled by this exercise were then put out to civil society organizations, business associations, and think tanks, as I will explain in the next chapter, for further deliberation, to validate them and to find solutions.

Harsh and the team of interns continued to support the widening consultation. They became an ad hoc 'lateral linking' organization to become a bridge across the boundaries within the Planning Commission, and also a bridge across the ideological and intellectual boundaries between the civil society organizations, business associations, and others who were now being drawn into a widening process of thinking together.

FIVE

WHEN THE PEOPLE SPEAK

The National Development Council, which is chaired by the prime minister, consists of the chief ministers of all the Indian states, with the prime minister and several key members of the central cabinet. It is the highest body in the country of all that direct the nation's development. The preparation of every Five Year Plan is preceded by the drawing up of an 'Approach Paper'. The Approach Paper lays down the principles that will be adopted in the plan and it highlights national priorities the plan should address. The Approach Paper must be approved by the National Development Council before the Planning Commission proceeds to develop the Plan.

The Planning Commission's charter, laid out in the Cabinet Note of March 1950 says that in order to be successful, the Planning Commission must 'enlist the association and cooperation of the people at all levels.' The Cabinet Resolution also says 'The Planning Commission will determine the nature of the machinery which will be necessary for securing the successful implementation of each stage of the Plan in all its aspects.'

As mentioned before, Dr Manmohan Singh urged the Planning Commission to become 'an essay (that is a force) in persuasion,' and not merely a writer of lengthy plan documents that people do not read. Several questions arose for the Planning Commission to consider: How should it enlist the cooperation of the people? At what stage should it associate the people in the formulation of the Plan to obtain their maximum support in the Plan's implementation? Should not their support be enlisted while formulating the Plan? Should the Plan be phrased in the language of the people rather than the terminology of economists (so that the people can comprehend it and be persuaded by it)? Would it not be better to include the voices and expressions of the people early on in the process?

The Planning Commission had begun to open up its planning process to inputs from stakeholders when it had framed the previous (the eleventh) Five Year Plan. Four regional consultations had been organized, in the North, South, West, and the East of the country, to which the state governments, business associations, and civil society organizations in that region had been invited. These formal, two-day meetings had enabled some opinions to be expressed. However, there was hardly any time for deliberation on the issues, nor an intent to debate them. The purpose of the meetings was, as far as many participants could gauge, for the Planning Commission to 'tick off the box' of 'Did you consult the stakeholders?'

The conduct of the National Development Council's meetings angered many chief ministers. They were made to sit in the well of the stately Vigyan Bhavan while the Chairman of the Planning Commission (the prime minister) sat on the stage above them, along with the deputy chairman of the Commission and the cabinet members who were in the Commission. Those on the stage talked to them. Then the chief ministers were given a few minutes each, strictly timed and with a buzzer to stop them, to make their remarks. When all of them had spoken, the meeting would conclude with statements from the stage. The most vocal chief ministers complained that there was neither the time, nor the intention to deliberate together.

Ms. Jayalalithaa, chief minister of Tamil Nadu, one of the country's wealthier states, said in a huff that she saw no reason to come to the Planning Commission to be told how to spend her own state's money, and she walked out of a National Development Council meeting after she finished her speech and told the media outside that the format was insulting and the meeting was a waste of time.

Narendra Modi, who was a three-term chief minister of Gujarat, another rich state that generated large amounts of resources internally, also had similar feelings about the Planning Commission. He, too, was openly critical of the shallowness of the participation in the meetings of the National Development Council, and the arrogance he perceived in the annual meetings of the chief ministers with the deputy chairman of the Planning Commission. In these meetings the chief ministers had to tolerate criticism and bad advice from Planning Commission officials who seemed to have a lot of numbers but little knowledge of conditions on the ground.

In the first months of 2014, the chief ministers of the states came for their last round of meetings to have their annual plans approved by the Planning Commission. At that time, Narendra Modi was campaigning vigorously to be elected as the prime minister of India, and was touting the 'Gujarat model' as proof of his ability to manage development. He came to his state's meeting with the Planning Commission.

The meeting began, as these annual meetings always did, with the state's chief minister making some opening remarks. Except that in Mr Modi's case, the remarks were always in the form of a very sleek, short video about the progress of Gujarat. The video was peppered with impressive numbers of the state's progress, some of which the Congress party's economists and spokespersons had been challenging publicly to counter his election campaign.

When the presentation was over, the deputy chairman of

the Planning Commission, Montek Ahluwalia, asked Mr Modi the question that he had asked all the chief ministers that had come to the Planning Commission in 2014. The UN had recently published statistics of the numbers of malnourished children in the world and India had come out very poorly, as it had for many years. Montek's point was that the statistics about India were a few years old and India must have made progress since then. He was compiling the latest numbers of the actual status on the ground from the states so that the Government of India could counter the poor impression created by the UN report. Therefore, he was asking the chief ministers what the latest numbers were in their states. He asked Mr Modi for the numbers in Gujarat. Mr Modi said that he would have the numbers sent to Montek immediately after the meeting.

The practice in these annual meetings with chief ministers was that, after the chief minister had made a presentation, each member of the Planning Commission would be invited by Montek to comment or ask questions. Some Members would rely on statistics given to them by their advisors within the Planning Commission and point out deficiencies in the state. In this meeting, too, two Members contested some information presented in the Gujarat video, saying that the Planning Commission had different information.

When he had heard all the members, Mr Modi turned to Montek. He said that it was odd that, on one hand, Montek wanted the state government's information to know what was really happening on the ground, and on the other hand, members of the Planning Commission did not trust that information and said they had better information! 'In which case,' he said, 'you should know what the state of malnutrition is and should have no need to ask the chief ministers.'

The chief ministers of the states were not the only persons dissatisfied with their interactions with the Planning

Commission. There was a growing demand from civil society organizations also that the Planning Commission's consultations with them should be less pro forma and deeper. Many civil society organizations came together on a common platform to demand more participation of people in the planning process. They called their platform Wada Na Todo Abhiyan (WTNA). Wada Na Todo translates as 'Do not break your promise'. Abhiyan is a 'campaign'. They wanted the Planning Commission to be accountable for the promises made in its plans. And they wanted it to live up to its promise, in its charter, to associate with the people and obtain their cooperation.

WTNA knocked on the doors of the Planning Commission in 2011 when it was time to formulate the Approach to the Twelfth Five Year Plan. 'How about consulting us?' they asked. My fellow member of the Planning Commission, Dr Syeda Hameed and I met with them. We came to an agreement about how the Planning Commission and WTNA could collaborate to bring in the voices of people, especially the most excluded and marginalized, to make the approach to the Twelfth Five Year Plan more inclusive.

The WTNA welcomed this move from the Planning Commission. They made the following observations in *Approaching Equity: Civil Society Inputs for the Approach Paper: 12th Five Year Plan,* their report of the consultation process that followed:

'The Planning Commission has, in a path-breaking move, approached civil society organizations to engage with them openly, formally and systematically and opened up the process for inputs into the approach paper (instead of sharing and seeking inputs after the draft approach is ready).

'Civil society groups feel this move is a key window of opportunity to actualize the shift of the planning process to a people-led one, make the 12th Five Year Plan inclusive, and create spaces for the most marginalised. There is also a need to institutionalise this process into a formal, systemic one.'

Both the Planning Commission and WTNA were keen to make the consultation process systematic and satisfying to both. WTNA claimed that hundreds of civil society organizations (CSOs) would be willing to participate in it if it was a more serious, better designed process than the previous engagements of the Planning Commission. (WTNA has recorded in its *Approaching Equity* report the names of 600 organizations and another 200 civil society experts who participated in the process that followed. The Planning Commission noted that another 200 organizations were also consulted in addition to those who came on the WTNA platform. Thus, the total numbers approached 1000).

How do you listen to hundreds of CSOs representing many diverse groups of citizens spread around the country, and a variety of issues? And do this in a short time because the Planning Commission would have to complete the Approach Paper within three months? How would sense be made of all the inputs that could be provided by these hundreds of CSOs? WTNA suggested that the consultation process would be much sharper if the Planning Commission was clear about the questions it wanted to consult the CSOs about. Fortunately, the Commission was ready with its twelve questions.

A meeting was convened of the leaders of WTNA with Planning Commission Members to design the consultation process. When they saw the list of questions, the WTNA said that they were good questions, and some of the WTNA leaders began to offer some answers there and then. I asked them to pause. The meeting was to design a large consultation process, and not to discuss the answers. 'Not yet,' I said. 'We want to hear the people's views.'

The person I had interrupted was offended. He claimed that his CSO represented over a million people. He knew what their opinions were. I asked how often the members of the CSO met. 'We meet all the time!' was the answer. I could sense the outrage that was building within him. How dare I doubt his credibility? But I pushed on. If the organization was having meetings frequently, it would be easy for it to include discussions of the Planning Commission's questions in meetings over the next few weeks. Would he please consider that? The riposte to that was quite swift. Would I, or some other members of the Commission come to the meetings? Surely it would be of more use for us to hear the people's views, than for him and the other leaders of his CSO because they already knew what their people's views were.

From this repartee emerged the need for all the CSOs to make their own process systematic and to prepare their calendars of meetings in which they would discuss the questions with their members so that the Planning Commission's Members could try and schedule their participation in some of them. A date was set by which the Planning Commission must have the submissions from the CSOs so that their suggestions could be considered before the draft Approach Paper was finalized.

The Planning Commission's members wanted especially to listen to the views of the citizen groups who were the most excluded from the mainstream, such as the dalits, tribal people, minorities, women, children, and the differently abled. There were many CSOs representing each of these groups of citizens. The members requested that the submissions from each of these groups should be consolidated by WTNA. A leader of a large CSO said that his organization would prefer to submit its recommendations directly, and other CSOs could do the same. That way the Planning Commission would have the benefit of many views, she suggested.

Thinking ahead, I wondered how the Planning Commission would consolidate the views of all CSOs representing women, for example. What if the views of organizations who knew the needs of women very well, as they claimed, were not aligned? On what basis would the Planning Commission make a judgement of what would be better for women? If the Planning Commission was inclined to go with one view and not another, it could be blamed for taking sides. And if the Planning Commission settled on a compromise which neither liked, both would accuse it of not understanding what was best for women!

My suggestion that the CSOs should thrash out their disagreements amongst themselves was received with some mirth. 'What world do you live in, Mr Maira? Do you know how difficult it is for two CSOs, with different ideologies, who have publicly disagreed, to agree with each other?' I persisted that the women of India would be served best if those who knew their needs could come to an agreement amongst themselves. And the same would apply for the other CSOs representing other citizen groups.

Later, when the consultations were over and the Approach Paper was published, WNTA's leaders met with the Planning Commission to do an 'after action review'. They wanted to give feedback on how the process followed could be improved in future. They said that the best contribution the Planning Commission had made was to insist that the best way in which the CSOs would serve their stakeholders would be for the CSOs to learn to listen to each other and find solutions together.

The CSOs were very disappointed when they read the Planning Commission's draft of the Approach Paper. They could not see their points-of-view incorporated in it. It seemed to them that the Planning Commission had not heard them at all. They requested a formal meeting with the deputy chairman of the Planning Commission so that they could convey their disappointment and also make another effort to get their points of view understood.

The deputy chairman heard them. He explained that the Planning Commission was not obliged to accept everything the CSOs proposed. The Planning Commission had to consider the views of others too, who were often not in agreement with the views of CSOs, and then make up its own mind about what was best for the country. Some CSOs alleged that the Planning Commission had a pro-Western and pro-business bias and was 'anti-people'. Others quietened these shrill protestors and supported the deputy chairman's position that the Planning Commission had to consider many points of view. However, they would have liked the Approach Paper to present the principal points of view and explain why, in the interests of the people, it was recommending one view.

Moreover, they said, the language of the Approach Paper was not easy for the CSOs and their members to understand. Could it not be made simpler? The deputy chairman's cursory response to this, that the Approach Paper was not being written for the benefit of CSOs and that it was addressed to people who understood planning language, annoyed many of them. If the Planning Commission would not even admit the need to engage the people in a dialogue for which it would have to adopt language they understood, there was no point in continuing the meeting. At this point the deputy chairman left the meeting.

The leaders of WTNA who had arranged the meeting were dismayed. So was I. We had hoped to build better bridges between civil society and the Planning Commission. Now there was a breakdown.

I offered to stay back and discuss how the process could be changed to achieve the objective for which WTNA and the Planning Commission had begun their innovative collaboration. While some of the CSOs left when the deputy chairman did, many others accepted my invitation to stay back and find another way to achieve our objective of co-creating a systematic process for better consultation between stakeholders and the Planning Commission.

It had become clear from the 'outside-in' review of the Planning Commission that I had been asked to do in 2010 that the Planning Commission should develop better processes to present the big picture of the country to citizens. It should provide a 'radar' view of the forces shaping the country, and where the risks and opportunities were, for making safer and faster progress. The radar view should be intelligible to people, or it will not guide them. What the CSOs had said was that they could not understand the relevance of much of what was in the Approach Paper made by the Planning Commission.

Statistics of GDP growth, fiscal deficits, and trade balances, and the language of economists in which the Planning Commission's principal documents are written, such as the Approach Paper and the Five Year Plan, is not intelligible to the vast majority of citizens.

For fifty years, every morning, the late R.K. Laxman told the powers in the nation what the common man thought about what they were up to. His daily cartoons were the most jargon-free commentaries on the development of the Indian economy. In 2004, R.K. Laxman graciously helped me select eight of his cartoons to include in my book, *Remaking India: One Country, One Destiny.* The pictures said much better what I was trying to say in words.

One cartoon showed a poor man reading a newspaper and proclaiming, 'Terrific progress! In growth rate, in industry, in exports, and in exchange reserves—what a change from the miserable situation we were in!'

Another shows two beggars outside the Stock Exchange watching many happy brokers come out. Says one beggar, 'Look, we are really fortunate—the Sensex must have gone up still further!'

A third shows an angry politician berating villagers

surrounding him, 'All the time you ask for drinking water. Don't you ever want to progress? I'm telling you I am giving you telephones.' Higher growth rates, rising stock markets, millions more cell phones.

Laxman's point was that the government cannot convince the common man that he is really better off with numbers like GDP growth and such macroeconomic indicators of progress.

The prime minister had directed the Planning Commission to reform itself, to become an 'essay (that is a force) for persuasion'. To persuade the people, it would have to change the language of its communications. He had also asked the Planning Commission to change itself from being a financial allocations body into a 'Systems Reform' Commission. Soon after the prime minister gave his directives, the deputy chairman had invited several people with experience in planning processes to brainstorm what new processes the Planning Commission could apply to prepare the Twelfth Five Year Plan. The process of 'scenario planning' had been recommended. Scenario planning is a 'systems thinking' based planning process. It recognizes all significant forces that are shaping a complex system and analyses their interactions. With this analysis, scenarios are prepared which describe conditions of the system in the future depending on the directions the forces may take. The condition of a country's economy and society is not shaped only by economic forces but by social and political forces also. For instance, citizens' expectations and their level of trust in the government are critical forces that impact the economy.

Quantitative predictions are not possible when the variety of forces is large and some of the strong forces are not quantifiable, such as citizens' trust in government, and when the ways in which they will interact cannot be converted into mathematical equations. Scenarios are not predictions. Scenarios describe plausible shapes the system can take depending on the directions of the forces. Furthermore, good systems analysis enables citizens to determine the consequences of their own actions on the outcomes. Thus, scenario planning can persuade citizens to support policies that will produce the outcomes they desire.

Scenario planning could be described as a process for citizens to find the wisdom that the theologian Reinhold Niebuhr said we must all seek. As I've mentioned before, he had said,

'God give me the courage to change the things I can; the serenity to accept the things I cannot; and the wisdom to know the difference.'

Scenario planning can induce wisdom. It points to strategies that must be courageously pursued to improve the condition of the complex system, which is the economy and the society, in which all citizens are participants.

I suggested to the CSOs that we may consider using the scenario planning process. Some of them had heard about the application of the process in South Africa in the 1990s, when the new government was sworn in after the abolition of Apartheid. The expectations of people in South Africa were very high, but the tensions within the country were very high too. A good process was required to analyse what the country's development strategy should be considering its economic, social, and political challenges. This strategy would have to be understood and supported by the citizens to create alignment amongst them, without which the country would be torn apart.

The South African scenarios were called the 'Mont Fleur scenarios' because the participants in the process met, quietly, in the small Mont Fleur hotel to consider the future of their country. The participants represented the contending stakeholders: the blacks and whites; and industry, civil society, and labour unions. They invited Adam Kahane, a scenarist from the Shell Oil company which was a pioneer in the use of scenario planning in the corporate world, to guide them through the process of scenario planning for South Africa. These leaders engaged in a deep dialogue. They listened to each other's hopes and to each other's suggestions. They developed a systems map of the territory of change that South Africa would have to traverse and what would be alternative paths through it. They evaluated the risks and opportunities along these alternative paths.

These leaders, who were (and would remain) competitors to each other outside the process, had developed a shared view of the world of which they were all a part. If in their eagerness to win their internal competition, they were to destroy their world, the victory would be not worth anything even to the victor. They realized that they would have to convey this view to their supporters too. They would need language that the people could understand. What better language than pictures and metaphors?

Therefore, they created memorable pictures of the plausible futures for South Africa and laid out the choices before the country. Each of these scenarios was supported by a simple systems' analysis that explained what forces would cause that scenario to emerge. The desirable scenario was called 'The Flight of the Flamingos'. In this scenario, the contending parties would squawk at each other for a little while, but then they would slowly take off together in formation. It was another image of the vision of the 'rainbow nation' that President Mandela evoked so powerfully to inspire cooperation. (The other scenarios, less desirable, were called 'Lame Duck', 'Ostrich', and 'Icarus'.)

Several people in that meeting of the CSOs with the Planning Commission, that seemed to have come to an impasse, volunteered to participate in a scenario planning exercise to shape strategies for the country's development if I were to organize it. Later, Indian business leaders also volunteered to join them. And leaders of Indian think-tanks engaged on strategic, trade, and environmental issues also came forward. Together they used the tools of systems thinking and scenario planning to shape strategies for India's progress.

Meanwhile, the official Approach Paper was rubber-stamped by the National Development Council, with cursory participation of the chief ministers. And this Approach then led into the preparation of the Twelfth Plan in much the same way that previous plans had been made.

SIX

MANY DANCERS, ONE DANCE

This was not the first time the process of scenario planning would be used to understand the forces shaping India and strategies for the country's progress.

The first time the process of scenario planning was applied in India to my knowledge was in 2000. Montek Singh Ahluwalia had been appointed a member of the Planning Commission in 1999. I was intrigued about what Montek would do. He had served many years in the World Bank until he came back to India and became a close advisor to Prime Minister Rajiv Gandhi in the freeing of the economy from central controls. Thereafter Montek, along with Finance Minister Manmohan Singh, was a member of the team that assisted Prime Minister Narasimha Rao in the reforms of 1991 that dismantled the edifice of industrial licensing and controls and opened up the Indian economy to foreign trade.

I wrote to Montek from the US where I was consulting at that time. I asked Montek what he expected to do in the Planning Commission, which continued as a central planning body, inconsistent with his beliefs that such organizations must be dismantled to free the economy. My consulting practice was focused on systems of strategic planning in conditions of uncertainty and on assisting large organizations to bring about transformational change. I mentioned to him that other methods of planning were being developed and applied, very different to the Soviet-style centralized control model that seemed to continue to drive India's approach to planning. One such new approach, I mentioned in my letter, was scenario planning and amongst the examples I mentioned to him was the Mont Fleur scenario planning that had been developed in South Africa a few years earlier. Montek was intrigued.

He suggested I try this new approach in India. However, he shortly moved to the International Monetary Fund (IMF). Meanwhile I planned to return to India in 2000 and, with the help of my friend Tarun Das, director general of the Confederation of Indian Industry (CII), enrolled others to develop scenarios for India.

A brief history of scenario planning is in order. Scenario planning was first applied by the US defence forces after the Second World War to design strategies for operations in uncertain environments. Military strategists have to envisage what may be happening *out there* and develop strategies to win regardless of what *may* happen. Scenario planning techniques were later applied in the corporate sector to develop strategies when the environment around the corporation is uncertain. There is great risk in investing large amounts of money on the assumption that the world will be progressing in a certain way. What if some developments out there change the scenario entirely? This was the question for the Shell Oil company, for example, when it was considering its strategies in the 1980s. Would the Soviet Union permit export of gas from its enormous reserves? If it were to, then prices of gas in Europe could fall sharply, making gas production within Europe much less attractive. The Soviet Union was a closed shop. What was going on within it was difficult to read. Shell used scenario planning and it got it right, whereas its competitors sank large amounts of money in wrong strategies.

South Africa was going through political turmoil in the

early 1990s. It was impossible to predict what its future may be. At that time, some business leaders in South Africa asked Shell Oil for help. Could Shell depute an expert in scenario planning—a scenarist—to help leaders in South Africa to imagine what their country could be and what would be good strategies to produce the best outcomes? Shell deputed Adam Kahane.

Adam had to adapt the scenario planning techniques that the armies and corporations had developed to the new situation he found himself in. The uncertainty for armies and corporations is in the situation *out there.* They want to determine how to move their troops and invest their resources out there. They would want to know what is happening in the Soviet Union: what is its internal situation—its politics and economics. In South Africa, the concern was with the situation *in here.* The situation within South Africa would be determined almost entirely by the actions and reactions to each other of people within the country. So what should the people within it do to produce the best outcome for themselves?

Adam adapted scenario planning to enable South African leaders to develop the best strategy for their own country. After South Africa, he was invited to apply these new methods of scenario planning in Guatemala and Colombia, other strife-torn countries. He also applied them to contentious public policy issues in his own home country, Canada. I found Adam and asked him to guide me to apply scenario planning in India.

Adam was very generous. He was intrigued about the possibility of applying scenario planning in India. He felt the scale and complexity would be much larger than in the countries he had worked in so far. I invited him to come with me. His commitments in other countries prevented him. Over cups of coffee and tea in his apartment in Boston, he shared his notes with me. He had developed a methodology and he offered his manuals to me free of cost.

The methodology required a group of diverse societal and political leaders to come together for three intense, three-day workshops spread over a few months with work to be done in between. Adam insisted that the commitment of this group to attend all the workshops must be obtained up front for the process to succeed. They would have to experience the changes in their own thinking, and in their relationships with each other, as the process unfolds. I told Adam that this would not be possible in India. Important people will not take three days off for a workshop. Even if they were to, their attendance cannot be assured. They will come in-and-out of meetings and may not show up at all even after they have confirmed their attendance. We would have to adapt his method to Indian realities.

I shared with Adam the wonderful experience I had in Quebec City, in his native Canada, where I had recently gone for a short holiday. On a beautiful summer day, in a charming square in the city, an accordionist was playing in a corner. A young couple passing through the square paused, and then began to dance. Some others who had been listening to the music, also joined them in the dance. The young couple moved on. Others who came into the square joined the dance. Some moved on. Others came. The dancers changed. The dance continued.

I told Adam this was the metaphor for the process we needed for India. For this we must know the essential notes in the music, or we must know what beat a drummer should provide to induce people to dance together. We must find the core principles of a method for scenario planning in an open setting, and not insist on every step being performed as prescribed. Adam and I agreed to collaborate in this search. I began the work in India. Adam and I corresponded and met many times subsequently. We compared notes and became very good friends. Many years later, Adam came to India to lead an unusual process of collaboration amongst leaders from government, civil society organizations, and corporations to understand the root causes and to find systemic solutions to the endemic malnutrition of children in India in spite of the country's impressive economic growth rates. That project too provided both of us with deep insights into the sources of contention amongst stakeholders in a system and means to engender better collaboration.

I began the scenario process in India using Adam's templates modified for Indian realities. Many Indians from different walks of life came together to try out this new approach for creating a strategy for their country. They included politicians, business leaders, civil society activists, and academicians. They also included women from villages in Haryana, weavers from Karnataka, college students from the Indian Institutes of Technology (IITs), and even homeless children who lived on the streets outside the New Delhi railway station. Though some persons had important positions in government, large corporations, and academia, everyone came in their personal capacities, as human beings and citizens who cared about the conditions in their country.

A common language was required in the meetings to enable such diverse people to be able to express their thoughts and be understood by others. Therefore, in an opening meeting all participants were asked to bring with them an object that represented for them the essence of India — its potential or its challenges — that they would like to express to others. Even a child can bring an object and so can a learned professor. And everyone could explain their objects in a few simple words.

Mr N. Vittal (then Chief Vigilance Commissioner) came with a bag of groundnuts. He said that the majority of Indians are poor people, but they have the sturdiness of a groundnut that can grow with little irrigation. He said a groundnut, with the seed inside, represents the regenerative capacity and the tremendous potential of India. He also felt that India and the problems of India, like groundnuts, were not difficult to crack: provided we could release the potential in the people with the little 'irrigation' they needed.

In another meeting, children living on the streets outside the Paharganj railway station in New Delhi presented their story in a play they enacted. It was their representation of what their life had been in the villages from which they ran away, and what their life was like in the city.

In another meeting, an entire wall of a large ballroom was covered with rolls of news-print paper, top to bottom, so that people could draw on it, and stick pictures on it, without damaging the fancy wall-paper of the ball room. Within two days, as many groups of people came into the room, listened to each other, interrogated each other, and synthesized ideas, the wall was covered with the images and ideas they had produced. Step-ladders were required to reach up towards the ceiling when the wall space lower down became crowded!

People walked around the room, looked at the thoughts on the wall, and began to make connections between ideas. They moved the pictures and words around to form clusters of related issues. At the end, a picture of the Indian system emerged—with its challenges and its potential.

India is often compared to an elephant. And a story is often told about how several blind men around an elephant had to each say what they could feel when they touched the elephant—one the leg, another the tail, and a third the trunk. Only by putting their impressions together could they understand what the animal really was. Similarly, many perspectives must be brought together to understand India. This proper understanding is necessary before one can make viable plans for India's progress.

The pictures of India that emerged from this first round of scenario building for India revealed insights into the models of leadership India needs and also better ways of organizing change in a large system with great diversity such as India. I will explain these models and ways when I present the three scenarios that emerged in the second round of scenario building for which these pictures provided valuable insights.

SEVEN

SHAPING THE FUTURE

By the turn of the millennium, India's GDP growth had begun to accelerate. Economists were projecting that India would become one of the world's three giant economies, along with China and the US, by 2040. Indian business people, economists, and policymakers were in a celebratory mood. India was shining. The future was ours.

However, some people were sceptical. They pointed out that economists' projections have an awful track record because they do not factor into their models the social and political forces that can change the trajectory of their economic extrapolations. They pointed out that in the early 1980s economists were comparing the US and the Soviet Union as the two largest economic blocs, and economists were expecting Japan to be the powerful economy of the 21st century — they even talked of a Japanese century. China did not even figure in their projections then. Yet, within fifteen years, the picture changed dramatically. There was no Soviet Union and Japan was in the doldrums. Instead China was the emergent power of the twenty-first century! So, how could one be sure of India's future trajectory? Did economists really understand what was going on within India, including the socio-political forces which would influence India's future?

The World Economic Forum (WEF) undertook to apply the techniques of scenario planning in 2005 to examine the future of the BRICs countries—China, Brazil, Russia, and India. The forum's scenarists asked me to help them develop scenarios for India.

The forum had organized a workshop in Goa to build the foundations for the scenarios. From its members, the forum had been able to enrol some executives of MNCs in India. It had also invited some Indian economists, who were friends of the WEF. The MNC executives had a limited understanding of the complex socio-economic dynamics of India. They were keen to learn from the economists who, as it turned out, had mostly a theoretical understanding of the country. Moreover, the economists were from the 'right' end of the ideological spectrum, and therefore, the perspective of economists from the other end, the 'left', was missing. Therefore, the pictures of India that emerged in the Goa workshop were sketchy and incomplete.

Meanwhile, the CII, which had provided the logistical support for the first round of India scenarios that I have reported, had independently proceeded since then to organize meetings around the country for diverse citizens to meet together to develop shared visions and collaborative plans for the country's progress. The CII had branded these meetings as 'Leadership Conclaves' and had enrolled me to design and conduct them. The first of these Leadership Conclaves had been held in Goa some time before the WEF scenario workshop. The next Leadership Conclave was scheduled in Jaipur soon. I suggested to the WEF that they request the CII for an invitation to the Jaipur Leadership Conclave. Since the CII was supporting the WEF's scenario work in India, the invitation was obtained.

The Jaipur Leadership Conclave was held in February 2005 in the lawns of the Rambagh Palace in Jaipur, under trees and amongst flowering bushes. The purpose of the Conclave was to provide an opportunity for emerging leaders from many walks of life to pause and reflect together on what they could do together to enable desirable changes in the country. The meeting was unlike any meeting that the participants had been to, they said. It was not a conference, it was an 'unconference', someone said, because it violated the conventional ways of conducting conferences.

Firstly, there was great diversity of vocations, ages, and life stories amongst the 100 participants. There were business leaders, politicians, bureaucrats, farmers, teachers, leaders of NGOs, students, journalists, homemakers, diplomats, and others. There were young students and retired cabinet secretaries. Women and men were in equal numbers.

Secondly, the physical ambience was different. Even though some very senior persons were present (the chief minister of Rajasthan, Ms Vasundhara Raje, participated), there were no high tables even for the plenary sessions, and no assigned seats. Even Ms Raje sat amongst the participants. All meetings were in the open under trees or garden umbrellas. The physical setting helped to create an ambience that made people venture out of their mental boxes and the positions of status that they had become trapped in.

Thirdly, the meeting was designed as a dialogue amongst participants rather than as a series of monologues that other meetings tended to be—there was no assigned time for speeches, nor any designated speakers. The only 'speeches' made were by me, as the moderator, to describe the purpose of the meeting and to lay down the protocols that the participants would follow to ensure that everyone would get an opportunity to be listened to if they had something to contribute. It was stated and accepted that the primary orientation at the Conclave must be to listen and learn, and not try yet again to convince (with arguments that are stuck in our heads and that we repeat at multiple forums).

Fourthly, there was a systematic progression of ideas, in

stages, from shared aspirations for the country, to analysis of challenges to be met, to sharing of insights about how the challenges may be met.

The WEF team from Geneva and London listened intently to the discussions. They heard voices of India that they could never hear in economists' numbers, or in seminars in five-star hotels, or in glossy consultants' reports—which were their usual sources of information about any country. When the scenarios of India, China, and Russia were presented at the WEF's annual meeting in Davos in January 2006, Alexander van de Putte, the director of the WEF's scenario project, said that the India scenarios were different. They were different because the process was different. The India scenarios had people's emotions in them, he said, and expressed their caring for their country.

Three Scenarios

Three scenarios of India's future emerged from the WEF-sponsored process that I facilitated. The first scenario was called BollyWorld (a spoof on 'Bollywood', the popular name for India's prolific movie industry). It was a combination of two worlds that were growing side by side in India. These worlds were described in pictures that had come from the first round of scenarios. One was a picture of peacocks strutting with little birds scrambling around them for grain. This was the story of the opening of markets in India. The goal of economic reforms is to improve the lives of the poorest people. Thus, in this picture, the courtyard is opened and grains are scattered for the birds to eat. The hope is that the little sparrows will get the grains. However, the pigeons are stronger and they get to the grains first. And when the peacock arrives, even the pigeons move aside. They will have to wait till the peacock has fed. This scenario portrays what happens when markets are opened. Those who already have the wherewithal to take advantage of new opportunities, who have some capital, or good education, or access to people in power, will get the benefits of opportunities first. Thus they will become richer and stronger. Others cannot access the opportunities as easily and so disparities in incomes grow. The rich show off their new wealth, the big cars they drive, the branded clothes they wear, and the huge mansions they live in. They are the peacocks.

However, there exists another vivid picture in the BollyWorld scenario. It is a picture of wolves prowling in the jungle. A picture of spreading violence in many districts of the country, and even in India's cities, side by side with the show of wealth. According to the WEF's scenarists, this combination of glamour and violence was like a Bollywood movie. In this scenario, India was becoming a BollyWorld. Good fun to watch from the outside but increasingly dangerous on the inside. A world that was not sustainable.

The tensions within, and the political reactions to them, could result in the second scenario called Atakta Bharat ('India stalling'). The picture describing this scenario had buffaloes wallowing in a pond with a little boy waiting outside. The buffaloes represent senior netas (leaders) holding important offices, and experts in many fields, who are expected to develop and implement plans to shape the future of the country. Such plans should produce results for the people, especially our children (represented by the boy waiting outside the pond) who are the future of the country. The netas and experts are expected to develop and implement plans for the future of the country. However, they cannot agree with each other. When one buffalo gets an idea and wants to move ahead, the others do not want to move. So the buffalo settles into the pond again. Then another buffalo gets an idea. But the first remembers that he had not received cooperation and so reciprocates by refusing to cooperate! Thus decisions are not made and progress is stalled. Meanwhile, the children of the country are waiting for education to be improved, and for healthcare and nutrition.

These scenarios were created in 2005. They predicted that BollyWorld could slip into Atakta Bharat. Fortunately, signs of another scenario of India were also emerging like little shoots of grass. It was observed that there were many local initiatives, and many entrepreneurs, who were improving their own conditions and the lives of the people around them. Though each of these initiatives may be small, their numbers were multiplying. Women self-help groups (SHGs), community water management programmes, producers' cooperatives, grass-roots innovators, millions of small scale enterprises— these bottom-up initiatives were transforming lives wherever they were lit up. This scenario of 'Fireflies Arising' and lighting up the darkness represented a changing India. The WEF scenarists called this scenario 'Pahale India' ('India first') because this was the process by which a democratic and diverse India would truly shine. A big power lit up by millions of fireflies.

The WEF scenarists had to present the scenarios to business leaders and economists at Davos. Such hard-nosed people would scoff at mere pictures. They would want numbers. The WEF commissioned two economic forecasting groups, the National Council of Applied Economic Research (NCAER) in India and the Oxford Forecasting Group in the United Kingdom (UK), to evaluate the scenarios in economic terms. The forecasters confirmed that while both BollyWorld and Pahale India would grow the economy to over 9 per cent GDP growth, BollyWorld would not be sustainable. It would deteriorate into Atakta Bharat and growth rates could fall to 6 per cent or less. On the other hand, fireflies of Pahale India was a sustainable model of high growth. Moreover, poverty rates would fall fastest in the Pahale India scenario since more people would be creating the growth. It would be a trickle-up and not a trickle-down process. The scenarios pointed to a sustainable approach for India's inclusive growth.

Scenarios are not predictions. They describe situations that will arise if the forces at play take a turn one way or another. They also suggest the actions that can be taken to prevent less desirable scenarios emerging and more desirable ones to come about. The WEF's India scenarios provided warnings for India's policymakers which were unfortunately not heeded. In 2005–06, with high GDP growth numbers, India seemed to be shining. The social tensions within India, which the BollyWorld scenario described so vividly, and which could result in an 'Atakta Bharat' if corrective actions were not taken, were ignored.

Economists have been finding it increasingly difficult to predict the future condition of the global economy or any country's economy. Very few economists predicted the global economic recession. Very few predicted the sharp decline in the Indian economy's growth. Many forces interact dynamically to change economic conditions. Globalization has connected many countries' economies together. What happens in one country will quickly infect other countries' economies. The collapse of Lehman Brothers in the US caused a global financial meltdown. The internet, 24X7 news, and social media can change 'moods' and 'sentiments' that can affect stock markets and create panics in foreign exchange markets as well.

Economists require models of the salient forces that shape an economy. They must have mathematical equations into which they can put values of these forces, which they can run on computers to compute what the state of the economy will be. The models of the Indian economy which India's economic planners had been using did not fit the economy any more. The shape of the economy had changed with the loosening of internal controls on the economy and with the increasing openness of the Indian economy to the world since the 1990s. A project was undertaken by the Planning Commission in 2009 to develop an up-to-date model of the Indian economy. Several economic research organizations in India, each of whom had a model of the economy, were invited to share their models, with the expectation that a combination of them could provide a more reliable guide to India's policymakers and economic forecasters.

Some economists admit they suffer from physics envy. They aspire to model complex socio-economic phenomena in the way physicists model natural phenomena. Physicists have methods to make good models of complex systems. Using mathematical equations derived from their models, they can make remarkably accurate predictions. Thus they are able to control the trajectories of rockets and the flight paths of satellites to land them on distant planets. There were two physicists in the Planning Commission formed in July 2009—myself and Dr Kasturi Rangan, former chairman of the very successful Indian Space Research Organization. The deputy chairman of the Planning Commission, Montek Ahluwalia, invited both of us to a meeting in which the economic research organizations presented their models and debated their features amongst themselves. He was curious to know if we could help to improve the structure of the models.

Dr Kasturi Rangan and I sat close to each other like friends in a strange forest, in the room full of economists with their equations and numbers flashing across the projection screens. We wondered what the models were trying to represent. We could not see the forest for the trees. Afterwards, Montek asked me for our impressions. I said I could do no better than reproduce the record of a meeting called by Kenneth Arrow and Brian Arthur, Nobel Laureates in economics in 1987.

Kenneth Arrow and Brian Arthur arranged a meeting of economists with physicists, including Nobel Laureates Murray Gell-Mann and Phil Anderson, to understand what economists may learn from physicists about the formulation of theories and models. The economists presented their models.

M. Mitchell Waldorp gives an account of the meeting in his book, *Complexity: The Emerging Science at the Edge of Order and Chaos (1992: 140):*

'And indeed, as the axioms and theorems and proofs marched across the overhead projector screen, the physicists could only be awestruck at their counterparts' mathematical prowess – awestruck and appalled. They had the same objection that Arthur and many other economists had been voicing from within the field for years. 'They were almost too good,' says one young physicist, who remembers shaking his head in disbelief. 'It seemed as though they were dazzling themselves with fancy mathematics, until they really couldn't see the forest for the trees. So much time was being spent on trying to absorb the mathematics that I thought they weren't often looking at what the models were for, and what they did, and whether the underlying assumptions were any good. In a lot of cases, what was required was just some common sense.'

In fairness to economists, I told Montek, economists must deal with a more complex world than physicists. Economics is a social science, which must understand and then model the behaviour of human beings. Human beings have feelings and passions. Fundamental particles, atoms, and molecules – the constituents of the systems that physicists model and represent in their equations – have no such qualities. They can be represented as pure quantities. Human beings are much harder to quantify. Therefore, the predictions from mathematical

*M. Mitchell Waldorp. *Complexity: The Emerging Science at the Edge of Order and Chaos.* Penguin, 1994.

models of economies are bound to go wrong when human fears and aspirations, which cannot be accurately quantified, change the condition of the system. What economists need is a method to explain a system with all the forces in it, including those that cannot be quantified. Scenario planning, founded on systems thinking, does just this.

After the meeting of the Planning Commission with the Wada Na Todo Abhiyan in 2012, many people with diverse backgrounds came together to develop scenarios of India's future to facilitate new, collaborative conversations amongst citizens and policymakers about India's future. They were aided in their efforts by the Centre for Study of Science, Technology and Policy (CSTEP) which developed the conceptual scenarios model into a more robust system dynamics model.

Inputs were obtained from many diverse people and sources of information, as mentioned before, to understand the forces that were impacting India's growth. There was an unmistakable voice of mistrust in government institutions, political parties, and businessmen. It seemed that all those so-called 'leaders' were in there for themselves. Who was there for the citizens? (It was like the picture of buffaloes wallowing in the pond while children are waiting outside it, in the scenario of Atakta Bharat).

This mistrust was leading to protests in various forms, from street demonstrations to public interest litigations, which were causing political logjams, and policymaking had become 'paralysed'. At the same time aspirations had been rising, of youth who wanted satisfaction of their desires faster, of middle class families who wanted better standards of living, of businessmen who were becoming used to making lots of money fairly quickly, and economists and international investors who expected the Indian economy to match up to China's growth rates. The rising expectations on one hand,

and the bottlenecks to progress on the other, were creating a potentially combustible situation.

Predictions of GDP growth rates must be based on the social, political and institutional forces within the country, which are often treated by economists as exogenous to their mathematical growth models. The systems analysis helps to locate the leverage points, which are those forces that affect the condition of the others. For India these leverage points lie in the condition of its institutions of governance and business. The quality of institutions has an impact on trust in government institutions and large businesses. Lack of trust in institutions increases impatience in society, and this leads to a political logjam, which in turn makes reforms that the system needs more difficult. Which then reduces economic growth rates.

The condition of external factors that impact India's progress is not easy to forecast. Therefore, the most important question for the country's policymakers is: what strategy will ensure that the country will be best placed regardless of these external uncertainties? Not surprisingly, India will be most secure in times of uncertainty if it is internally cohesive and strong. Therefore, when the world around is changing, the plan for India must concentrate even more on institutional reforms within.

The leaders of NGOs, business, government, and think-tanks who had come together to develop the scenarios of India to guide the country's plans went deeper to examine what kind of institutions India should develop and what should be the thrust of its policies. They found three levers.

A. *The approach taken to inclusion: The 'how' of inclusion.*
A principal challenge for economists and policymakers all over the world has become how to achieve 'inclusion' along with economic growth. Two contending approaches

are evident. One emphasizes 'redistribution': taking from those who have more, and giving to those who do not have enough. The other approach emphasizes creating more access to opportunities, so that the less well-off can increase their incomes faster and also contribute to growing the pie. At one end the emphasis is mostly on 'handouts'. At the other end are determined efforts to generate more opportunities for good livelihoods accessible to all sections of society. Scenarios can project the consequences of choosing one course over the other.

B. *The approach to 'governance': to strengthen local, community-based and collaborative governance rapidly.*

When systems seem to be 'not in control', the instinct is to centralize. However, if the reasons for slow results are that the diversity in the system is very large and therefore, solutions must be locally adapted, and also that there is not a strong centre, then it may be best to strengthen local governance rather than try to impose central control. At one extreme, the way most things are run is, in effect, 'central' and 'siloed'. At the other, local rural and urban governments are effectively in charge of their affairs with vigorous participation of local citizens. In a devolved structure with power closer to where results are required, and with different parts of the system working collaboratively, adaptation and learning are faster too.

C. *The 'theory-in-use' towards energy and environmental solutions (as well as enterprises): Big projects or more community-based solutions and enterprises?*

Local and smaller solutions can create more ownership and responsibility for the use of resources and also ensure more equity in distribution of benefits. The argument against this theory is that scale is required for more efficiency. Innovations in networked enterprise designs can enable the benefits of both, local ownership as well as the benefit of scale where required. On one end, big is good is the dominant paradigm. At the other end, only small is beautiful. Network-based models of enterprises and governance systems combine the strengths of both.

Three scenarios, once again, of India's future

The analysis revealed three plausible scenarios of India. They can be described under the headings 'Muddling Along', 'Falling Apart', and 'The Flotilla Advances'. These scenarios result from different configurations of the three 'theories-in-use' — the three levers mentioned before.

Each scenario is an explanation of what the condition of the country will be if the forces that affect it play out, or are caused to play out, in one way rather than another. The National Council of Applied Economic Research (NCAER) was commissioned to create a macroeconomic model and project the quantitative outcomes of the scenarios.

Scenario 1: The Flotilla Advances

This is an optimistic scenario under the assumption that the government would successfully drive key structural policy reforms and their effective implementation. Decentralization and good governance policies will improve the efficiency of the public delivery system and address the supply side bottlenecks. Under a positive policy environment, the investment climate would also be positive, with significant net capital inflows and healthy growth in private investment, both being drivers of economic growth.

Under this scenario, the government is able to meet its medium-term fiscal goals, with the deficit coming down to around 3.6 per cent of GDP by 2015–16 from the current level of 5 per cent of GDP.

The overall GDP at constant 2004–5 prices is projected to grow by an average of 7.8 per cent during the Twelfth Plan period (reaching 9.3 per cent by 2016–17). Across the production sectors, the services sector is expected to register higher growth of 9 per cent followed by the industry sector at around 7.1 per cent and the agriculture sector at 3.3 per cent.

Scenario 2: Muddling Along

Under this scenario, India would initiate some reform measures to encourage investment. However, the business environment continues to remain weak as the reforms may cover only a narrow set of issues. Net invisible receipts and foreign direct investment (FDI) inflows will remain weak due to domestic policy uncertainty. The stock market (BSE Sensex) will continue to show poor returns in this scenario and there will be more pressure on the rupee to depreciate against the US dollar. Both central and state governments will miss the opportunities to control unproductive expenditure.

The overall GDP growth is estimated at 6.0 per cent per year for the Twelfth Plan period, a decline of 1.8 percentage points over the Flotilla Advances scenario. The decline in GDP growth has occurred in the services and industry sectors due to the decline of private investment in these non-agriculture sectors. There is also less impact on poverty reduction as the growth effects are smaller.

Scenario 3: Falling Apart

This is the most pessimistic scenario among the three, both in terms of economic performance and policy environment. This scenario reflects a situation where the government would be unable to undertake key policy reforms. Subsidy levels are not stabilized. The policy logjam, especially relating to investments, witnessed in the latter part of the Eleventh Five Year Plan would continue. The tax revenue growth will remain weak with the implementation of key tax policy reforms, such as Direct Taxes Code (DTC) and Goods and Services Tax (GST), being delayed further.

The allocation of resources in the health and education sectors would decline as a ratio to GDP from the current levels due to resource constraints. The public sector investment both in agriculture and non-agriculture sectors would decline substantially as compared to the pre-crisis level.

In this scenario, the overall annual GDP growth for the Twelfth Plan period was estimated at 4.8 per cent, a decline of 3 percentage points over the Flotilla Advances scenario. The GDP growth rate declines across all the sectors because of a significant fall in investment (both private and public) and a rising fiscal deficit.

It took almost a year from the time the scenarios were made for NCAER to complete its modelling and calculating. During this time, the conditions in the country were slipping from those described in the Muddling Along scenario, which is where the country's governance seemed to be when the scenario process commenced, to those in the Falling Apart scenario. GDP growth rates were already slipping below 5 per cent, down to the levels NCAER calculated for the Falling Apart scenario.

Governance, Implementation, Total Productivity

The most significant number amongst NCAER's computations was the substantial difference, of around 3 per cent per annum, in the rate of growth between the Flotilla Advances and Falling Apart scenarios. This difference arises due to *internal governance* matters, not external conditions which are the same for both scenarios. (The Muddling Along scenario, also with the same external conditions, is in between the two.) This 3 per cent difference is the result of reduction (or improvement) in the 'total productivity' of the economy by changes in effectiveness of resource use. To improve total productivity, resources should be directed towards desired outcomes and there should be less waste too in their use. Devolution of responsibilities for planning and implementation to lower levels of the system—in the states, and in local urban and village management bodies, and building capacities at these levels for good planning and management, are a large opportunity to obtain total productivity improvement of the Indian economy. The country must tap these sources of human and institutional energy much more vigorously for faster as well as more inclusive growth.

These three scenarios along with their explanations, with the images of boats, buffaloes, and fireflies, were published by the Planning Commission on its website. I reproduce a picture that was published. In this picture there is also an image of a key. The key indicates the levers for change—the 'theories-in-use' for governance that must be altered—to enable the desired scenario to emerge: the one with the flotilla advancing and fireflies arising.

Three of the levers on this key have been explained already. There is also a fourth lever, a very critical one, which will be explained in Part 3.

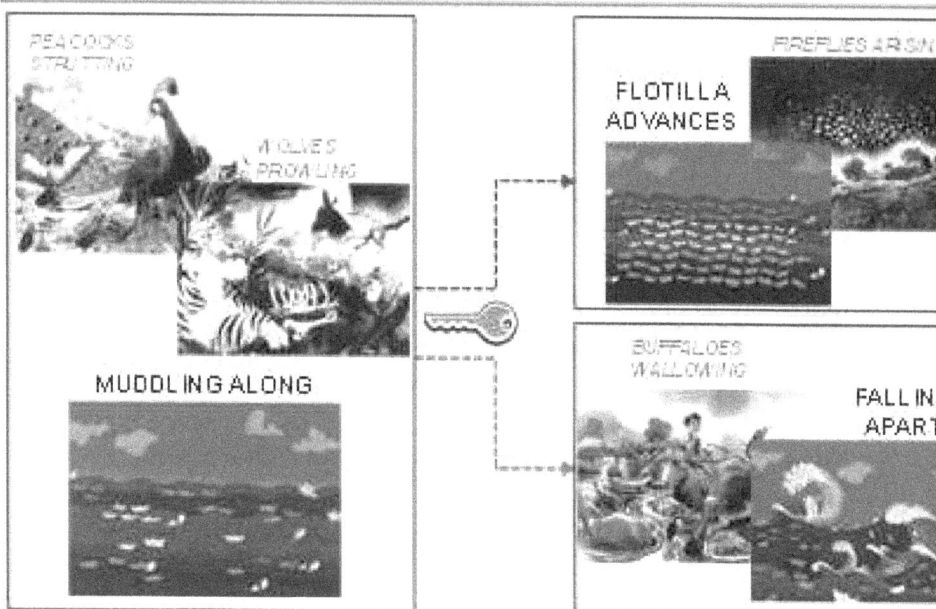

Figure 3: Three emerging scenarios of India.

EIGHT

THE CHANGE BEGINS

Scenario planning was a desirable 'Plus' to the Planning Commission's legacy processes of preparing Five Year Plans. Scenarios provide the 'radar' that stakeholders wanted the Planning Commission to provide governments in the states, private sector business organizations, independent civil society groups, and others, to direct themselves to produce the best results for the whole system, that is, India, of which they are all a part.

Meanwhile, the old planning processes embedded in the Planning Commission's organization lumbered on. All the official energy of the Planning Commission was used in these legacy processes; for the Planning Commission's divisions and its members to write the chapters of the Twelfth Five Year Plan within the page-lengths they were assigned; for debating with the central ministries to estimate what the expenditure budgets should be; for determining what percentage of cut should be applied to their estimates to fit into the overall resources available to the government which were becoming constrained with the declining growth rate of the economy. The Planning Commission was stuck in the rut of allocating money and making budgets rather than reforming the system for which the scenarios provided a broad blue-print.

When the draft of the Twelfth Five Year Plan was finally put together in late 2012 (many months after it should have been ready, which should have been before the Eleventh Plan ended in March 2012), its contents did not feel right to the deputy chairman and the members of the Planning Commission. The country was churning. Anti-corruption movements were roiling the system and exposing the rot within. The media was stridently taking up issues of public safety, especially of women. Citizens were demanding improvement of public services, and more accountability from the government. Inflation was rising unabated and growth was declining.

To use the metaphor of an aeroplane in flight with citizens abroad: the citizens were warning the captain about foul smells and grating noises in the aeroplane's systems, and about the aeroplane losing height. A plan made by the country's highest planning institution must acknowledge these problems up front. It should explain, in a credible and transparent way, what the causes of these problems are. It should point to the need for a plan to address these issues of governance (even if it could not yet offer a plan) rather than drifting along, discussing macroeconomic numbers in its opening chapters, as previous plans had. The citizens will be reassured if the pilot acknowledges, at least, that he is aware of the problem.

A debate took place within the Planning Commission. Should the Planning Commission be talking about governance issues at all? Is not the economy the only remit of the Planning Commission? This debate, at this late stage of preparing the plan, was surprising. Even if the remit of the Planning Commission is to be only the growth of the economy, surely the Planning Commission must point to all the important factors that affect economic growth? Besides, had not the prime minister charged the Planning Commission with a reform agenda of becoming a 'Systems Reform' Commission rather than a budget-making body? Moreover, the credibility of the forecasts of the government and its economic advisors (which included the deputy chairman of the Planning Commission) had become very low. They had been predicting for over a year that the economy was turning around and that the next quarters' numbers would be better but the decline had continued.

The government, and the Planning Commission with it, was caught in a trap. Should it admit that conditions in the country were not as good as they should be? If it did, it would be blamed. However, if it tried to convince citizens that conditions were good when they felt they certainly were not, citizens would say that the government was out of touch with reality.

Should not the Planning Commission be an objective guide to the government and above partisan politics? This was a question that troubled some Members. If it was, should it not present the facts to the government and the people? How could it be trusted otherwise? Ms Sudha Pillai, the Secretary of the Planning Commission, had been very recently sworn is as a member of the Planning Commission as well. She asked the Members to recall the oath they had taken when they were sworn in. (I remembered the oath very well because I had to renounce my US citizenship and obtain my Indian citizenship again just so that I could be sworn in as a member of the Planning Commission.)

We had all sworn our allegiance to the constitution of India, and had taken an oath that 'we will do right to all manner of people in accordance with the constitution and the law, without fear or favour, affection, or ill-will.' We had not sworn to serve the government of the day, she said, but to serve the constitution and the people of India.

Montek built up courage at this stage to propose to the prime minister that the scenarios should be placed in the opening chapters of the Twelfth Five Year Plan. The scenarios described the 'big picture' more fully than macroeconomic numbers could alone. They explained what forces were shaping the country's economy, especially the condition of governance. They did not predict a growth rate; rather, they pointed out to what would be required to be done to reform the system and improve the growth rate. The growth rate would improve *if* these things were done. That is what a good strategic plan does: it tells you what you must do to get the result you want.

However, the titles of the scenarios, which were in the language of the citizens who had helped to shape them, were not acceptable to the PMO. They were changed into more acceptable official language for the Plan document. 'The Flotilla Advances', was changed to 'Strong Inclusive Growth'; 'Muddling Along' to 'Insufficient Action', and 'Falling Apart' to 'Policy Logjam'. Nevertheless, even the mention of the scenarios in the opening chapters of the Plan document, amongst all the numbers of growth rates, saving rates, and so on was a breakthrough. It was a 'Plus' to the planning process.

The system analysis supporting the scenarios had pointed to architectural changes in the country's systems of governance that were long overdue. The states could not be, and should not be dictated to by the centre. They should be given more freedom to devise solutions for their own progress and for the welfare of their citizens rather than the 'one-size-fits-all' solutions in centrally sponsored schemes which had been growing in scale during the previous ten years. The states must form, with the centre, into a flotilla that advances together, with each state's ship led by its own captain and crew, and all guided by a radar that the Planning Commission would provide. Institutions of local governance, in the cities and in rural districts and villages, must be strengthened so that planning is done by the people for the people.

Reform of governance and planning institutions

A new central government was elected by the people of India in May 2014. They had become greatly disenchanted with the incumbent political dispensation and government. A new government was ushered in to reform the system. The first institutional reform Prime Minister Narendra Modi announced, on the anniversary of India's Independence Day, 15 August 2014, from the ramparts of the historic Red Fort, was the abolition of the Planning Commission. On 1 January 2015, the cabinet resolved to form a new institution to replace it, the NITI Aayog—the National Institution for Transforming India.

The Resolution says that the country 'requires institutional reforms in governance'. The charter of this new institution is very clear. It must change the processes of planning in the country, to make planning more participative and bottom-up, and to make the states partners in the planning process rather than supplicants to the centre for funds. The Resolution says:

'Governance, across the public and private domains, is the concern of society as a whole.'

'Governance encompasses and involves everyone.'

(There is) 'great scope for participative citizenry.'

The charter of the NITI Aayog demands changes in the architecture of governance along the vertical dimension, as well as the horizontal (lateral) dimension. On the vertical dimension, it demands devolution. It charges the new NITI Aayog to:

'Evolve a shared vision of national development priorities with the active involvement of the states.'

'Develop mechanisms to formulate credible plans at the village level and aggregate these progressively at higher levels of government.'

Along the horizontal dimension, the Resolution requires

the NITI Aayog to create systematic processes for collaboration. It charges the NITI Aayog to:

'Provide advice and encourage partnerships between key stakeholders and national and international like-minded think tanks.'

'Offer a platform for resolution of inter-sectoral and inter-departmental issues in order to accelerate the implementation of the development agenda.'

The responsibility of the country's central planning institution, which will now be the NITI Aayog, for improving processes of governance and planning was firmly settled.

Jobs and livelihoods

In addition to reform of the governance system, the scenario analysis had also pointed to the need to change the focus of policies for inclusion, from 'hand-outs' to those left behind to faster creation of employment and opportunities for better livelihoods. The analysis explained that this was the only way in which growth would become genuinely inclusive and sustainable. Hand-outs to compensate those who are not sufficiently included, though they are often required, is not a good way to enable people to stand on their own feet, and nor is it an economically sustainable way for the country.

India's GDP growth, though impressive, has not been converting growth to jobs and livelihoods as fast as many other developing countries have. Some international comparisons, such as the Boston Consulting Group's SEDA (Sustainable Economic Development Assessment) framework had suggested that a unit of GDP growth in India was producing fewer jobs than a unit of GDP growth in India's peer group—its neighbouring countries, countries in Southeast Asia and the BRICs countries. This pattern of growth is not socially and politically sustainable for India with its huge population of youth—the source of the potential 'demographic dividend' to its economy.

While the Twelfth Plan was being put into its final shape, many reports had begun to appear in the media about India's 'jobless growth'. Many within the Planning Commission had been saying that it was perhaps the most critical issue to focus on while making plans for the country. Readers may recollect that the off-site of the Planning Commission's officers in 2010, which came up with a list of the country's twelve principal challenges, had highlighted this challenge. The officers had attempted to rank the twelve challenges in terms of their immediate importance. There was a debate about whether the challenge of faster generation of employment (and enhancing skills) should be put on top of the list. In the end, 'Enhancing the capacity for growth' was placed on top, to focus on improved mobilization of domestic and foreign financial resources, public–private partnerships, and so on.

When the Plan was in its final drafts, it was noticed that while the discussion of the capacity for growth was well placed in the opening chapters, as it usually had been, the focus on jobs slipped attention. The question of how more jobs and livelihoods will be generated was scattered into other chapters and its focus was lost. The three chapters in which generation of employment appeared as a central issue were the chapters on manufacturing, tourism, and construction. In a telling comment on how Five Year Plans were drawn up in the Planning Commission, the chapters on tourism and construction were almost dropped because the length of the plan document had to be reduced! These subjects were the tips of the tail in the document and could have been easily cut off, because there were no significant divisions in the Planning Commission dedicated to them who would demand their inclusion. Here was another illustration of how the Planning Commission's structures distorted its processes and how its past had been putting blinkers on plans for the country's future.

In its last few months, after the Twelfth Plan was prepared and approved, some members of the Planning Commission suggested to the deputy chairman that the Planning Commission would serve the country well by leaving a note, before remitting office, for the next deputy chairman and members of the Commission stating what we had learned about how the Planning Commission should be reformed. Some even felt that the prime minister, as chairman of the Planning Commission, would do well to make this note public, to show the people that the government was well aware of the need for institutional reforms and that it had not been asleep at the wheel.

As a part of this proposed note, a list of 'lenses' was made through which we recommended that the new Planning Commission should make the mid-term appraisal of the Twelfth Plan, which would be the first major task for it soon after it was formed. We suggested that, rather than doing a chapter by chapter review of progress, progress should be assessed from the perspective of the critical outcomes required by citizens. On top of this list of lenses was the subject of jobs, employment, and livelihoods. How well was the country progressing to create sufficient numbers of good jobs and opportunities for its youth? How could the pace of job-creation be accelerated?

NINE

DISCOVERING OUR WAY

The forecast made by economists in Goldman Sachs in 2001, that China's and India's economies were destined to become the largest economies in the world along with the US, within the first half of the twenty-first century, had excited the imaginations of many people. They recalled that the two Asian giants, China and India, had the largest economies in the world until the eighteenth century. Thereafter, the economies of European countries had grown very rapidly as they industrialized and then colonized many countries around the world. The most significant story of industrial growth and colonial expansion undoubtedly was Britain's industrial growth and its rule of India. As European powers expanded, China and India became industrial backwaters and their economies languished.

In the excitement of imagining the restoration of China and India to their historical pre-eminence, a crucial statistic was often overlooked. Goldman Sachs had projected the total GDPs of countries to produce its rankings as economists invariably do. China's and India's economies were expected to become huge, vying with the US economy, and well ahead of all other countries, because these two countries had huge populations: over a billion persons each. The next largest country by population was the US, one fourth their size. All other countries were much smaller.

When the sizes of their populations are also factored into the global GDP forecasts and incomes per capita are considered, another story emerges. I present a chart showing changes in per capita incomes along with GDP growth that was prepared shortly after the BRICs forecasts of GDP growth began buzzing around the world.

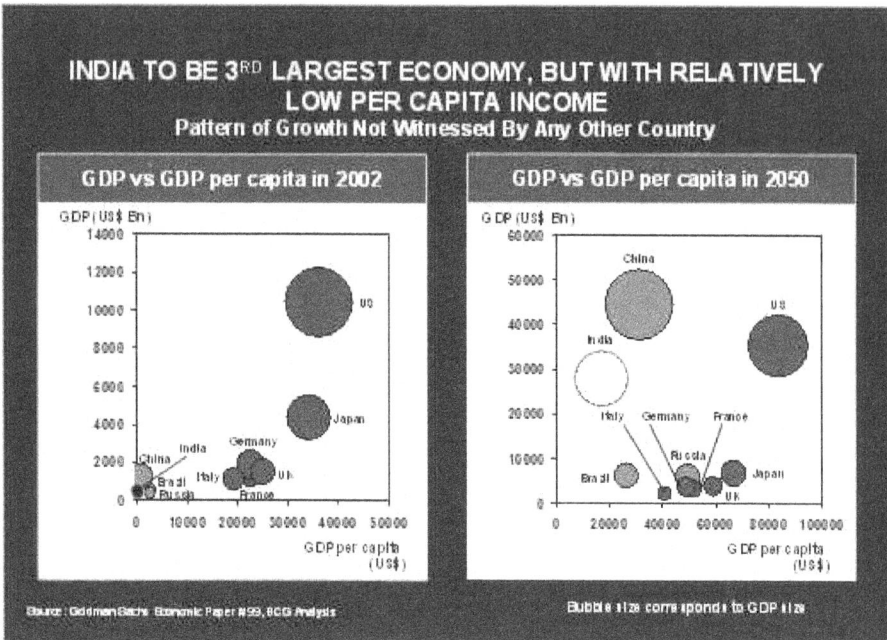

Figure 4: Projections of GDP and citizens incomes.

The story of economic growth between the eighteenth and twenty-first century had followed an upward curve. As a country's GDP increased, its position moved up along the vertical axis. At the same time, per capita incomes would also increase, and the country's position would also move right along the horizontal axis. China's and India's economic growths will follow the same pattern. However, the extent to which per capita incomes will increase in China and India with increases in their GDP will be much less, because the huge size of their GDPs is mostly a result of their having large populations. Therefore, as the chart shows, they are outliers on the curve. They will be very large economies but with many very poor people compared to Organisation for Economic Co-operation and Development (OECD) countries. The economists said that India's growth, following the rapid growth of China, would be propelled by a 'demographic dividend' to the economy, because India would have the largest numbers of young people in the world. What was often not highlighted was that the demographic dividend is not the straightforward result of a large population of young people. The young people must have incomes, through employment or through their enterprises. Their savings and consumption from their incomes will produce the demographic dividend to the economy. The key to economically and socially sustainable economic growth is the rapid creation of jobs and enterprises along with GDP growth. Without jobs, rising bubbles on the chart will be punctured: the projected growth cannot happen.

Economic growth in India has accelerated since the economic reforms of 1991. However, job creation has not kept pace with the growth of India's young population. A major cause of slow growth of job creation in India has been the weakness of its manufacturing sector, in glaring contrast to China's. China and India, two poor countries with populations exceeding a billion persons by the end of the twentieth century, began reforms of their economic policies around the same time in the last quarter of the twentieth century. China has been much more successful. By the turn of the millennium, not only was its economy four times as large as India's, its manufacturing sector (at 35 per cent of its economy compared with India's, which was 16 per cent of India's economy) was eight times as large. International economists say that China's economy has grown *because* its manufacturing sector grew.

They also say that the Indian economy's weakness in creating jobs is because its manufacturing sector has not grown enough.

As mentioned before, the prime minister, Dr Manmohan Singh, was very concerned about this. When I joined the Planning Commission, he had asked me to give special attention to develop a strategy to grow India's manufacturing sector.

It was very tempting to imitate what China appeared to have done to achieve the remarkable growth of its manufacturing sector. Large coastal areas had been transformed into buzzing factories, employing millions of people. The minister in charge of Industry in Dr Manmohan Singh's cabinet, Mr Anand Sharma, decided that India must set up similar large industrial estates and that this would be India's new 'manufacturing policy'. He proposed to set these up as self-governing enclaves not encumbered by the country's irksome laws regarding labour and the environment. He expected these areas would attract a lot of investments and would enable India to increase the share of its manufacturing sector in the GDP from 16 per cent to 25 per cent.

Dr V. Krishnamurthy, chairman of the National Manufacturing Competitiveness Council, was dismayed by the minister's plans. The council had been meeting with industry leaders in India for some years to determine what strategies for India's manufacturing sector should be. He was of the view that while the creation of large manufacturing zones may have been a good strategy for China, it was not a good strategy to grow India's manufacturing sector.

The first hurdle would be the acquisition of large tracts of land for them. China and India have historically followed different strategies regarding land ownership. In China, all land belonged to the state, whereas India had given land ownership to small farmers. Therefore, acquisition of land for industry had become a very contentious issue in India. It would take a long time to aggregate the large tracts of land required for the proposed industrial zones, whereas in China it could be done very quickly.

The idea of exempting large areas of the country from national laws to attract investment was problematic too. It recalled the special enclaves that Indian kings had given to merchants from Europe along India's coast. Great political opposition could be expected to the policy.

The third problem with this strategy was that, by focusing on some special areas which would be provided world-class infrastructure (and in which many Indian laws would not apply), not much would happen to grow jobs elsewhere in the country in the meantime. Inequalities within the country, along with differentials between the 'backward' areas and others, already a matter of great concern, would increase. In fact, one of the side-effects of China's policy of focusing only on some special coastal zones, which became factories to the world no doubt, were the 'three divides' that China's policymakers became acutely aware of in the early years of the new millennium. These were: the divide between the eastern part of China which developed faster and western parts of China which were developing more slowly; the divide between the coast and the interior; and the divide between urban and rural China.

India had promoted small and medium industries in all states since the advent of industrial planning with the country's Second Five Year Plan in the 1950s. When the new national manufacturing policy was being formulated in 2010, there were many pockets of industry all around the country which could be developed further. Dr Krishnamurthy asked me to accompany him to a meeting with the industry minister. Dr Krishnamurthy and I suggested to the minister that the stimulation of industry by relieving constraints, and the creation of an enabling regulatory environment, must be a prime thrust of India's manufacturing strategy. The minister agreed that the new manufacturing policy which he proposed to announce very soon would have two parts. One would be the thrust for large national investment and manufacturing zones, which would be the flagship programme of his policy. The other part would be the stimulation of manufacturing industries all around the country, which he asked me to prepare.

India and China, two giants amongst countries ranked by populations, began long and difficult journeys in the middle of the twentieth century, across a turbulent stream to the same destination. Both want to reach prosperity for their billion-plus citizens.

They entered the stream from different places. A difference in their starting conditions was the ways in which their national governments were formed after the Second World War. Mao led a violent revolution. 'Power,' he is reputed to have said, 'springs from the barrel of a gun.' Mahatma Gandhi led a peaceful movement for India's independence. India promulgated a constitution guaranteeing many fundamental rights to its citizens. It also created a strong and independent judiciary which could check the government whenever it infringed citizens' rights. Freedom of speech was guaranteed in India's constitution, and India's Supreme Court confirmed, in a landmark decision, that the right to property must be protected also. On the other hand, China abrogated all power to the state—to the Communist Party in fact.

When starting points are different, the courses that travellers take must be different even if the destination they aim to reach is the same. The map for one traveller's journey cannot be a useful map to guide the other. Therefore, to follow the way China had created a large manufacturing sector would not be a good guide for India. The Chinese government did not have to contend with owners of land, or with the rights of labour, when it created its large industrial estates. The Indian government would have to.

When the Chinese economy grew, quite remarkably too, the Chinese government began to give labour some rights to quell rising unrest in the large factories and industrial estates. It is easier to give something, than to take something people already have. Not unexpectedly, the policies to create large national investment and manufacturing zones in India, to emulate the Chinese zones, ran into difficulties. The acquisition of large tracts of land proved problematic. The proposition to give special exemptions from national laws in these estates faced opposition.

Deng Xiaoping, the leader of China's remarkable economic transformation, was a practical man. He said that the colour of the cat did not matter so long as it caught the mouse. He also said that China must cross the stream by feeling the stones underfoot. The feet moving along the stones are the doers—in the case of industrial policy, they are the industrial entrepreneurs. They have to negotiate over the stones, which are the constraints on their progress. Policymakers, sitting in the head of the body, above the water-line, must pay attention to the signals the feet give them about the constraints and opportunities they are sensing. Then the policymakers must signal to the rest of the body to shift its weight to enable the feet (and the body) to progress safely. Progress cannot be made when the policymakers are not tuned to the signals from the ground, and when they have their own views in the air about which way the body should proceed. Then there is great risk of the body tripping. China's manufacturing sector, and with it China's economy, had progressed remarkably. In comparison, India's manufacturing sector had progressed much more slowly. It seemed to have stumbled along the way.

Other nations that industrialized rapidly, such as Japan, Taiwan, and Korea, had adopted the same strategy, of connecting the feet and the head — industrial entrepreneurs and policymakers, in processes of policy-shaping, experimenting, adjusting, and learning to make the whole system progress. The quality of the interactions between the stakeholders and policymakers enabled the improvement of the competitiveness of their industrial sectors. In Germany too, whose industrial sector has proven to be sustainably competitive, the cooperation between industry, unions, and government policymakers is noteworthy.

I proposed that a systematic process should be initiated to engage representatives of industry and officials responsible for the making and implementation of policies relating to industry to develop policies for India to grow its manufacturing sector and create more jobs. This would provide the connection between ground-up and top-down learning, to connect the feet with the head, in a dynamic process of policymaking.

The country needed to create 100 million additional jobs in manufacturing within ten years, the seemingly audacious goal of the manufacturing policy. To achieve this goal, enterprises would have to grow in many sectors, and all round the country too. Past policies of import substitution, which may have dampened overall growth, did induce the creation of manufacturing capabilities in many sectors — automobiles, chemicals, steel, machinery, textiles, electronics, and others. Unfortunately, Indian manufacturers had been experiencing many constraints: in government policies, poor infrastructure, and weak institutions. Rather than doing a top-down 'picking of potential winners', an approach to industrial policy which has often been criticized for making bad choices, a more democratic, bottom-up approach was adopted. Let all associations of enterprises in any industrial sector make their cases for what they can do and what support they would need. Then practical strategies could be distilled from these inputs.

As many as twenty-six working groups were quickly

formed: sixteen focused on specific sectors, and ten on issues that affected all of them, such as the business regulation environment, human resources, and land. A systematic process was required to ensure that all these groups worked to a rhythm so that their work would be coordinated and policies could be distilled in a short time. A small team was required to design and conduct this participative and systematic process. This was the task for the Paradigm Consulting team, Sriram Ramchandran, Varoon Raghavan, and Arjun Nath, who I have already introduced to readers in Part 1.

The flotilla of twenty-six working groups was steered by the team of leaders of the working groups. In its very first meeting, this steering committee, which included CEOs of some of India's largest manufacturing companies, such as Maruti-Suzuki, Tata Steel, and L&T, and secretaries of ministries responsible for various industrial sectors, agreed that it would not be enough to make a plan. The steering committee should also examine what would be required to implement the plan. The country had produced many Five Year Plans before. They hardly ever produced their stated outcomes. Therefore, there would be little point in producing yet another plan which would not be implemented effectively.

It was suggested that the process of the 'Three Whys' should be applied to get to the root cause for the slow and incomplete implementation of projects and plans. In this process, often associated with the Japanese approach to Total Quality Management, which many CEOs were very familiar with, one should ask 'why' a condition exists. When the answer is found, the underlying condition causing this condition is now known. Then one should ask 'why' this other condition exists. And so on, keep asking 'why' until one comes to a root cause.

The steering committee agreed that India had an implementation problem, not a planning problem, or even a major resource problem. Projects were stuck. For example, money had been attracted to invest in large power projects, such as Ultra-Mega Power Plants (UMPPs), and other large industrial projects, such as the mega coastal steel plant that the Korean company, Posco, planned to set up. Implementation of these projects was stuck in bottle-necks. Policies were stuck. Bold new policies, such as the policy to open up the multi-brand retail sector to foreign investment, were stalled after they were made. Reforms were stuck. For example, for over twenty years both employers and unions had been demanding the modernization of the country's labour laws, but it was not yet done.

The steering committee and the flotilla of twenty-six working groups preparing strategies to grow India's manufacturing sector were composed of a diverse set of people, including government officials, academic researchers, representatives of business associations, and many experienced leaders of manufacturing enterprises. A refrain often heard in the meetings from the leaders of manufacturing organizations was to 'be practical'. 'Please understand the real constraints,' they would say, 'before jumping to theoretical solutions. The energies of entrepreneurs must be released. They are tied up in too many constraints. To be practical, you must find the most binding constraints and focus on relieving those, rather than going after a whole laundry list of constraints or, even worse, focusing too much energy on less important constraints.'

One can learn a lot about constraints by listening well to those facing the realities on the ground. Lots of data is not required to understand what matters to them. I recall a presentation made to the Planning Commission by a senior economist of the World Bank. He had gathered reams of data from Indian statistical agencies, and combined this with information from satellite surveys of geographical locations of enterprises in India. He presented his charts and pictures. His conclusion was that enterprises tend to cluster along roads! Some economists in the Planning Commission seemed impressed with the vast amount of data he had accessed and by his analysis. However, I was unimpressed. I said that if one had run a manufacturing enterprise, or listened well to a few people who had, one would understand the practical reasons for a manufacturing enterprise to establish itself close to transport infrastructure.

'Go to the real place, listen to the real people, understand the real thing', was the practice instilled in young managers joining TELCO in Pune from management schools. Leaders of the manufacturing enterprises on the steering committee followed the same practice in their organizations. Several scientific methodologies have been developed to locate the most binding constraints on improvement of the performance of a manufacturing system and these have been applied by many enterprises in many parts of the world to improve their competitiveness. These methods include the 'Theory of Constraints' developed by Eli Goldratt, and Minimalist Manufacturing developed by Professor Jaikumar of the Harvard Business School. Minimalist Manufacturing goes further than the Theory of Constraints to locate the distortions caused on the smooth running of a system by controls that supposedly should improve its performance. It points to controls that should be removed and which are the minimal, essential controls that should be retained: thus its name Minimalist Manufacturing.

Sriram Ramchandran, the founder of Paradigm Consulting, the start-up team that was assisting me in managing the flotilla of working groups and its steering committee, who I have introduced to readers before, had worked with Professor Jaikumar (as had I). Together, Sriram and I assisted the steering committee to get to root causes of constraints from the information provided to it from the working groups.

The steering committee found that the root causes of bottlenecks in almost all cases were contentions amongst stakeholders which were not resolved, and confusion amongst agencies who should coordinate with each other but were entrenched within their own silos. These bottlenecks had reduced the 'total factor productivity' of the Indian economy. Moreover, when many projects were stuck, investors were not willing to put more money into projects in India, no matter how glowing the future of India was according to macroeconomists such as the authors of the BRICs report.

V.S. Naipaul wrote *India: A Wounded Civilization,*in 1977, in which he had found, amidst the bureaucratic sloth in the country, an oasis of hope and confidence when he visited the Tata factories in Pune (which I have referred to in Part 1). After the strings on the Indian economy began to be untied in the 1980s, he wrote *India: A Million Mutinies Now* in 1990. In this book, he observed how the spirit of entrepreneurship was spreading around the country.

Someone in the steering committee said that if Naipaul were to write another book on India in 2011 its title would be *India: A Million Bottlenecks Now!*

When the root-cause problem was found, a solution for it had to be found too. The search for a solution to India's endemic problem was the genesis of the idea of the India Backbone Implementation Network (IbIn) which, with scenario planning, is another potential 'Plus' for planning for India's future. The idea of IbIn will be explained in Part 3.

Part Three

Learning to Work Together

◆

There are always three sides to every story:
your side, the other side, and the truth.

Unknown

The romance of democracy is that somehow the result will come out the
way you want, but everything we know about democracy is that the result
comes out the way the people want.

Jonn Mueller

ONE

COLLABORATING AND COORDINATING

India has an implementation problem.
The country must improve its ability to produce outcomes with limited resources. Progress is being impeded by myriad bottlenecks that are resulting in wastage of resources of time, money, and human capacity. The bottlenecks are at all levels: in the cities and districts, in the states, and in the Centre. A root cause analysis of these bottlenecks, done by the steering committee that developed the manufacturing plan for the country, revealed that unresolved contentions amongst stakeholders—in projects, policies, and programmes—were a prime cause. The contentions are often kicked upstairs for resolution from above, which creates bottlenecks in central coordinating capacity. Increasingly, these contentions are taken to courts to resolve them, which is very time-consuming. Therefore, they must be prevented from arising, at the root, with systematic processes for cooperation amongst the relevant stakeholders. This will improve the speed of implementation and reduce wastage of resources.

India and China are often bracketed as the two Asian giants. They are very different. They have different histories and different political systems. India has been a vibrant, noisy democracy since its Independence in 1947. China has been ruled by an authoritarian political monopoly, the Chinese Communist party. No doubt China's economy has grown much faster. Comparing China's and India's trajectories of development, many economists say that democracy may be an impediment to economic growth, and that development must precede democracy. Entering the new millennium, India was mid-stream in its journey of development, having entered the stream from the side of democracy. Turning around mid-stream to take another path from a different place would be very risky if not impossible. History cannot be unwound.

By 2012, Indian citizens were complaining loudly, through the media and on the streets, that politicians in Parliament and ministers in the coalition cabinet were behaving like the buffaloes in the scenario of Atakta Bharat. They were quarrelling amongst themselves while the country was demanding progress. Citizens had also begun to complain that the officials of the Planning Commission were wallowing in their own pond, out of touch with the lives of the common people outside it.

It would be too simple to blame only democracy and coalition politics for the inadequate progress of the country. The problem is deeper. It is caused by applying a wrong theory to the management of complex systems. When a problem is complex, the presumption is that some people at the top will have to solve it, and the more complex the problem is, the greater is the requirement for more experts in many fields to solve the problem, according to this theory. The experts from different disciplines bring their own perspectives, their own special knowledge, even their own jargon. Agreements amongst them are not easy. When they become too busy in debates amongst themselves, and are out of touch with realities and with the people on the ground, they seem to people like buffaloes wallowing in a pond, while the children are waiting outside the pond for progress to touch their lives.

There is a key at the centre of the picture of the three scenarios of India presented in Part 2. The key contains strategies to reach India's aspirational scenario of the Flotilla Advancing and Fireflies Arising. Three levers in this key have been explained. These were:

A. The approach to 'inclusion' in growth, to privilege policies for the growth of jobs and opportunities for good livelihoods for everyone, over policies for hand-outs and compensations for those excluded from growth.
B. The strengthening of local, community-based, collaborative governance.
C. More community-based environmental solutions and more small enterprises

The three levers reinforce each other. Local governance and community-based solutions are good seed grounds for small, start-up enterprises. Together they can create more livelihoods.

There is a fourth lever too. In fact, if this lever does not function, the others may not function.

Contentions that are stalling the progress of the country are not only amongst the people at the top. There are many disagreements amongst the people on the ground too. Therefore cooperation is required, not only amongst the big buffaloes, but amongst the people too. Indians are much too argumentative many say. They are neither able nor willing to collaborate with each other, nor able to come to agreements easily. Perhaps it is our culture, many say. And cultures are very difficult to change. So be it: 'chalta hai'.

But what if the problems of poor collaboration and poor coordination were not only cultural problems but management problems too? This was the question asked by the steering committee for the manufacturing plan. Could not the problems be reduced by applying good methods for collaborative decision-making and participative planning? Perhaps such methods for dialogue, consensus-building, and collaborative action could be found from other countries which were also democracies, the committee suggested.

The steering committee suggested that the introduction of systematic methods of collaborative planning and implementation must become a national campaign. A model of a process to improve a nation's ability to get things done is available in the Total Quality Movement in Japan. In the 1960s and 70s, techniques for group working to achieve zero defects and on-time delivery were disseminated throughout the country. Their application turned Japan from a producer of cheap, flimsy products into the hallmark of quality, and even premium pricing in many industries. The contribution of the Total Quality Movement to the Japanese economic miracle cannot be overstated.

Total Quality Management (TQM) was a movement for bottom-up change in Japan. Simple tools for diagnosing the root causes for poor performance of a system or process, and then designing and monitoring experiments to improve performance were put into the hands of front-line workers in industrial and service organizations. The practice of 'small group activity' was introduced at the same time, whereby a group of workmen, whose work was inter-connected, was given time off every week for them to meet together, use the tools, and make improvements to the performance of that portion of the system that they could change together. Visitors to Japanese factories in the 1970s were struck by the charts alongside the production lines prepared by the workers to monitor their team's performance, and by the spaces provided to them for their weekly meetings. The workers were expected to be in charge of their team's quality and were provided the tools and facilities to manage it. In most factories in Europe and America, industrial engineers and quality inspectors designed processes and made changes to them and workers had merely to do what they were told to do.

The Japanese approach to quality developed a culture of responsibility for one's work, and of continuous improvement, throughout an organization. The improvement of an organization's performance, and of Japan's performance thereby, was everybody's business. Together they could produce the change in national standards which separately they could not. And together they did.

The new tools and new practices of TQM were developed in many places in Japan. They were developed within corporations such as the Toyota Motor Company. Toyota's TQM-based 'just-in-time' production system was described by researchers in MIT in the US as 'the machine that changed the world' because it compelled automobile producers in the West to imitate Toyota's methods or face extinction. The new tools of TQM were developed by academicians too, such as the renowned professors, W. Edwards Deming and Kaoru Ishikawa, and others in the Japanese Union of Scientists and Engineers (JUSE) who promoted their use, observed the effects, and refined them.

TQM was not imposed on Japan by a central authority in the government. Its tools were developed by many. They were voluntarily adopted by organizations to catch up and stay ahead of each other. The movement for the adoption of TQM methods was accelerated by competitions to reward the small groups in companies who made the most improvements, whose winners were given national recognition. The radio and other media also played a role in disseminating the tools and methods. TQM 'infected' Japan and transformed it, for the better.

As the demand for TQM tools and services increased in Japan, many providers of these services grew, in the form of consultants and training programmes provided by industry associations and others. Thus a large 'market' for TQM methods developed in Japan, with demand and supply growing together. Some of the providers of these services found markets outside Japan too, in the US, Europe, and even in India.

Its tools were not 'culture-specific' to Japan: they were transportable across nations. Their use spread within some industries in India in a similar way to Japan—as an infection rather than a top-down imposition. TQM infected some organizations in India in the 1990s, especially in the engineering industries, and most of all in the auto parts industry. Japanese teachers and consultants were brought to India by these early adopters. Those who were infected, such as many Indian auto-parts producers, did very well. Indian auto-parts producers won more Deming prizes for quality (the highest honour in the world for quality) than any other industry in the world outside Japan. They broke into markets in the USA and Europe, where they became preferred suppliers of many sophisticated parts, and they made a lot of money too!

TQM methods are founded on 'systems thinking' and 'systems acting'. They require an examination of all constituents of a system to understand their inter-related causes and effects. And they require members of a team to work together, to align their actions to produce the best results for the performance of the system. The analysis made by the steering committee for manufacturing applied the quality management technique of asking the 'Three Whys' to get to the root causes of India's implementation problems. This had revealed that India needed a TQM-like approach to incorporate more systems thinking and more collaboration to reduce bottle-necks in projects and development programmes.

The team assisting me in the search for tools and methods that would improve implementation in India were the young managers in Paradigm Consulting. They were tucked into the room in the top floor of Yojana Bhavan, with the one table, one chair, one sofa, and the one whiteboard. There was no hierarchy within the fluid team. They developed methods for collaborating with each other, leveraging the best abilities amongst themselves to push along many projects simultaneously. No silos. No hierarchy. Sitting within the Planning Commission with its rigid internal organizational walls, they were becoming a living example of the spirit of collaboration across boundaries that was required in the Planning Commission (and for India) to get things done.

The team studied the national rollout strategy of TQM in Japan and also looked around the world for other examples of systematic methods of improving capabilities to collaborate and get things done in Korea, Germany, Brazil, Sweden, and the US. They were assisted in this search by the World Bank's Trade and Competitive Industries Division and by the GIZ (Deutsche Gessellschaft fur Internationale Zusammenarbeit), the German government's international development arm.

The World Bank needed to change its own methods of assisting developing countries when it came to assist India to improve its industrial growth. India needed the World Bank's money less and less as its own economy grew. Therefore, the bank's traditional products were not useful for India. Nor was the bank inclined to give any money to national governments for industrial development which, it insisted, should be done by the private sector. Therefore the only assistance that the World Bank could give to India's government to grow manufacturing and industry was to help it develop a better 'industrial policy'. But there was a problem with this within the bank. Since the Washington Consensus in the early 1990s, the World Bank had been preaching that 'industrial policy' was a bad idea. So how could a division in the World Bank go against the prevalent ideology of the bank and assist the Planning Commission and the Indian government with its industrial policy?

I presented the analysis the Planning Commission had made, of what India needed to accelerate the growth of its manufacturing industries, to officers of the World Bank's Trade and Competitive Industries Division, who offered to help. They agreed to help me find methods for improving implementation of complex programmes and projects that other countries were using, which we could learn from and adopt in India.

I knew several officers of GIZ in India who were doing very good work with several government ministries. They reported to me that GIZ had done an internal study of its developmental work around the world to understand why some projects worked out very well while others did not. They found that a common factor in the successful ones was the systematic engagement of all stakeholders in the project to win their cooperation. They said that GIZ was converting these insights into a teachable set of tools and methods for its staff. I audaciously asked them to give these methods to the Planning Commission so that we could disseminate them in India! These tools were graciously given to us and then customized for India in a package called 'IndiaWorks High Five'. IndiaWorks High Five is explained in the India Backbone Implementation Network's Knowledge Compendium, on its website, www.ibinmovement.in.

Now I am getting ahead of myself. I must explain the concept of the India Backbone Implementation Network which was germinated in the Planning Commission.

TWO

THE INDIA BACKBONE
IMPLEMENTATION NEWORK (IbIn)

Many people had been saying that the Planning Commission should focus on implementation. During the consultations with stakeholders for preparing the Twelfth Plan, many had suggested that rather than preparing another Five Year Plan, the Planning Commission should focus on implementation of its plans. Some even suggested it should be converted into an 'Implementation Commission'.

The Planning Commission's Members wondered how they would accelerate implementation if they were not given the authority over those who had to implement. The implementation of most programmes had to be done in the states, but the Planning Commission could not be given authority over the state governments. In fact, state governments were pushing for more freedom from central control because they were constitutionally responsible for producing outcomes for their citizens. Similarly, the central government ministries, which were also responsible for the implementation of plans drawn up by the Planning Commission, objected to the interference of the Planning Commission on constitutional grounds. Their ministers were accountable to Parliament and to the citizens, whereas the Planning Commission was not even a constitutional body — it had been formed only by an executive order.

The idea of improving the implementation of projects and programmes in the country by better collaboration and coordination was a very interesting one for the Planning Commission. It would enable more efficient utilization of resources and faster production of outcomes, which the Planning Commission was concerned about. Therefore, the idea of providing those who had to implement—the states and ministries—with the tools required, and to thereby improve implementation in the country, was a logical one.

This was a new paradigm for the Planning Commission which was accustomed to making things happen by wielding its authority over others. It derived its authority from its power to allocate money. In fact, recommendations by some expert committees that the Planning Commission should no longer have powers to allocate finances and that it should concentrate on providing strategic guidance was creating great angst in the Commission. The chief ministers of states would not be required to pay obeisance to the Planning Commission every year. Officers of the central ministries would not have to hang around in the corridors of Yojana Bhavan pleading for allocations and approvals.

The paradigm of serving the states and the ministries seemed to be a very new idea for the Planning Commission. It was not clear to the deputy chairman and officers of the Planning Commission how they would go about inducing the states and ministries to use better methods. They accepted my idea of forming only a small catalytic group to grow a movement of change, like Total Quality Management in Japan, as theoretically right. However, the Planning Commission's systems and staff were not equipped to work in this new paradigm. In fact, when a budget of only Rs 25 crores over five years was proposed for setting up the small nodal cell to seed the movement, many officers of the Planning Commission were incredulous! How could such a small amount of money produce the large effect that it promised? Controlling and catalysing are different paradigms. The Planning Commission's 'theory-in-use' of how things are done had always been the control paradigm. It found it very difficult to understand how a catalytic group works.

Montek Ahluwalia, the deputy chairman of the Commission, understood the dilemma very well. Once again he said to me that the idea was a good one and it would have to be implemented with resources outside the Commission because the Planning Commission would not 'get it'. Here, too, like the scenario planning process, a new process run by outside resources (and without demanding any financial support for it from the Planning Commission!) would have to be added as a 'Plus' to the Planning Commission's capabilities to reform it.

The Paradigm Consulting team of young managers in the room on the top floor of the Yojana Bhavan was already available to form the catalytic node of the India Backbone Implementation Network. They had helped to create the idea and understood it well. They operated in the new paradigm of a catalyst, rather than as an authority. They fitted the specifications of the nodal cell required for the IbIn network. Since the Planning Commission did not have to pay their salaries, which were paid by their sponsoring organizations, they could get going without waiting for lengthy approval processes in government.

There was one remaining constraint—space for the team! The room in Yojana Bhavan was beginning to get over-crowded. Besides, whereas one chair and one sofa were adequate when there were just two or three on the team, now there were five and soon there could be more. The Planning Commission could not officially provide another room or any more furniture. So the Planning Commission entered into a partnership with India@75, a philanthropic organization supported by the Confederation of Indian Industry (CII). India@75 agreed to support the new idea, initially by providing space for the nodal team within the CII office in Gurgaon.

The members of the team were fast-track managers from leading Indian corporations. They may have been accustomed to having their own cabins in their companies' offices. However, CII could not provide enough rooms, and nor did the team want them. CII prepared a fine office for them with work tables separated by low dividers. When the team moved in, it requested CII to remove even those dividers. Because they had become very accustomed to working seamlessly without any walls between themselves!

The infant idea for improving implementation required a name. It was christened the 'India Backbone Implementation Network'. Why these four words? 'India' and 'Implementation' are obvious since the purpose of the idea was to improve implementation in India.

The word 'backbone' represents the key capability that is required to improve implementation in India. The backbone, with the spinal cord through it, enables the body to coordinate the movements of its several limbs—the neck and head, the arms, and the legs. When the backbone and spinal cord are severely injured, the body can lose its ability for coordinated movement. During the brainstorming to find a name for the idea, someone playfully pointed out that, like Indian gods and goddesses who have many limbs, India is probably the most diverse country in the world. Therefore, India would need a stronger and a more supple backbone for its internal coordination than any other country.

The fourth word 'network' explained that the movement would not be an 'organization', with a hierarchy. It would have many partners and many projects connecting with each other laterally, not hierarchically. The four words together became the name of the idea: The India Backbone Implementation Network.

The India Backbone Implementation Network was publicly launched by the deputy chairman of the Planning Commission along with India@75 in New Delhi in April 2013. Many supporters of the IbIn network came to the launch function. These included the World Bank and GIZ, and many others who were inspired by the idea of the India Backbone Implementation Network and had come forward to support it.

The launch of the India Backbone Implementation Network was preceded by a workshop. Change-makers from many dozens of organizations in India, who are empowering people by creating institutions and by providing them with the skills to improve the world for themselves and others, participated in this workshop. There was a diverse set of organizations. They included the Self Employed Women's Association (SEWA), the Project Management Institute, Krishi Gram Vikas Kendra (KGVK) from Jharkhand, United Nations Development Programme (UNDP), the World Bank, and GIZ, and many others. They were delighted that my friend, Adam Kahane, who had facilitated the Mont Fleur scenario process in South Africa in the 1990s, and then worked in many other countries subsequently to introduce methods of collaborative scenario planning, came to India to facilitate this workshop.

Since its launch in April 2013, the idea of IbIn has grown. Many projects have been underway incorporating the IbIn philosophy and tools, which can be accessed on the IbIn website, www.ibinmovement.in. In the following chapters I will explain three IbIn projects to give a flavour of the IbIn idea and the movement for collaboration and coordination that it has begun to catalyse.

Many journeys of change and learning ran into each other, and ran together, to codify the disciplines for converting contentions into collaboration, and confusion into coordination, so that the intentions of plans could come to fruition through implementation. One was my own continuing journey. There were also the journeys of the start-up team which had expanded and morphed from Paradigm Consulting into the starting node of the India Backbone Implementation Network. I have already mentioned the names of some of these remarkable young Indians. The others were Abhinav Patwa and Anjali Birla from Tatas, Manish Meena from the Mahindras, Shipra Bhalla from the Axis Bank, Surbhi Ogra from the ICICI Bank, Alok Sinha from Larsen and Toubro, and Pragya Tiwari from GIZ. They engaged in projects for collaborative planning and implementation in cities, in industrial clusters, and in research projects to find and distil the best tools, the ones that should be widely disseminated. We joined the journeys of change and learning of people in other countries, who too are researching and applying methods to produce better outcomes through collaboration amongst stakeholders—our partners in Germany, Malaysia, the US, and many in India.

The start-up team was designed to be a fluid team, with some joining as others were leaving. The idea of the IbIn start-up team was like the dance in the square in Quebec City that I had described to Adam Kahane when I was adapting his structured methodology of scenario planning to an Indian culture. Some dancers left, others joined, and the dance continued. People changed, IbIn continued.

Everyone learned too. Here is what some of the young members of the start-up team said.

Arjun Nohwar said: 'The most interesting aspect of this journey was seeking out a variety of specialists and ecosystem partners who had relevance to what we were trying to construct, and how every additional interaction with them helped us absorb an additional capability/approach/idea, thus helping translate the concept of IbIn into reality.'

Anjali Birla said: 'For the first time in many years, with IbIn, I took a step back. It sounds funny because for any young consultant or management graduate, life is all about 'getting ahead'. Yet, working with IbIn I was forced to take a step back after every action to think, reflect, and capture the learning—such an underutilized yet powerful tool for self-development.'

Alok Sinha said: 'Working at IbIn helped me develop a systems approach to work; now, instead of quickly jumping on to the stage and offering solutions to a problem, I have developed the habit of taking a step back and spending time in understanding the system in which the problem exists. This I regard as a very significant addition to my problem-solving capabilities.'

And Ajith Francis said: 'My deepest learning at IbIn was inculcating the habit to listen to what others were saying and taking time out to respect what they were saying as well as understanding where the other person was coming from.'

THREE

MAKING IT EASIER TO 'MAKE IN INDIA'

M y father had to start life all over again after the Partition of Pakistan from India in August 1947. He found himself on the wrong side of the border, in Lahore, where he had established a very successful manufacturing enterprise, and where he and his younger brothers and families lived in a large house in Model Town. He had to leave all that behind. He came across the border and worked as the General Manager of the Nawab of Rampur's engineering company for a few years until he was allotted a small piece of land to start a factory in Govindpuri, in the Meerut district of Western UP.

His factory was amongst many other small factories, mostly owned by refugees like him, including one owned by his uncle, who too was a refugee, as our entire family was. There were no schools in Govindpuri, and I went to a boarding school in the hills, and later to St Stephen's College in Delhi. I would come home for my holidays, and then I would see my father's business progressing, slowly and with great difficulty.

Often he would go to the district headquarters in Meerut to meet government officials, and sometimes to the state capital in Lucknow, which was a long trip and kept him away from his factory for a few days. He had to wait for long durations of time to get appointments. When government officials, such as the factory inspector and the labour commissioner, visited

Govindpuri, all factory owners and their managers would be in a tizzy. These officials had great powers to interfere with the factories' operations, and often did. Getting government permissions and satisfying the demands of government officials took up much of my father's time, when he desperately needed to get machines to run, train workers, and establish a sales network. When I was finishing college, mentally preparing to sit for the civil service examinations, my father was very pleased. He would like to come and sit beside me on the other side of the table, he would laugh and say, where the officials sat while small business owners waited and worried outside their offices!

I did not join the government so my father could not get that satisfaction. I joined Tatas and was involved with the setting up of a very large green-field factory in Pune. Many permissions were required from many government departments for that factory too. However, they did not distract me or other senior managers. We were focused on the work of the factory, while some junior officers went to sort out matters with the government departments in Pune and Mumbai.

The small fellows

The business regulatory environment can have a great impact on the performance of business enterprises, especially manufacturing enterprises which have many more issues with land and buildings, pollution, and factory safety, than service enterprises do. The regulatory environment affects all enterprises, but it affects small enterprises most of all. Owners and managers of small enterprises are hands-on entrepreneurs with the skills necessary to run their operations. Every moment that the owners of small enterprises have to divert to dealing with government functionaries are moments taken away from the functioning of their enterprises. Thus, the performance of their enterprise suffers and their growth is affected. Owners of small enterprises have no one to whom they can delegate the dealings with government officials. In fact, even petty government officials expect to be waited on by the owners of these enterprises, whereas they hardly expect to meet top executives of the large companies, as I found during my many years in running large factories.

The World Bank would like all governments to pay attention to the quality of the business regulatory environment in their countries because it affects the growth of enterprises and the creation of jobs. Therefore, the World Bank publishes an annual ranking of the ease (or difficulty) of doing business in all countries. India has consistently been ranked among the worst performers amongst all countries. In 2014, India was ranked 142nd out of 189 countries. The Narendra Modi government has correctly chosen improvement of the ease of doing business as the principal thrust of its 'Make in India' strategy.

When I joined the Planning Commission in July 2009, the prime minister asked me to concentrate on finding ways to make the manufacturing sector grow faster. In my first month in the Planning Commission, I was invited by the Secretary of Micro, Small, and Medium Enterprises (MSME), to a meeting the minister of MSME had called with associations of MSMEs from around the country. There are hundreds of these associations. The secretary had invited the leaders of about two dozen of the largest associations and they had listed their myriad problems for the minister. They said they had been pleading for the resolution of these problems, year after year, with very little effect.

The minister said the prime minister was very keen to resolve the issues of MSMEs because he appreciated that they were the backbone of the manufacturing sector. The prime minister had agreed to meet the associations for half an hour in the following week. The problem the minister was having with the associations, which he asked me to help him resolve, was that the prime minister could meet only six representatives, along with the minister and the secretary. Who should these six be? And what would they say in the brief time they had with the prime minister that would be the fairest representation of the myriad issues of the MSMEs around the country?

It became very clear that a systematic process was required to analyse the principal constraints of the MSMEs, and also a better process for resolving them since previous efforts had not produced results. The prime minister agreed to set up a high level task force led by his Principal Secretary, of which I would be a member, and the Secretary MSME its secretary. We would engage with the associations, and with the many government organizations that MSMEs have to deal with, and collaboratively get to the key issues and find solutions for them. This work, which took almost a year to complete, gave me insights into the challenges MSMEs face and also the difficulties in resolving many of them.

A fundamental problem in resolving the constraints of MSMEs was that they did not have any high level forum in which their issues could get attention. Whenever the government wants to consult with industry, a dozen of the largest industrialists will be invited by the prime minister, finance minister, or industry minister: the likes of Mr Ratan Tata, Mr Mukesh Ambani, and Mr Kumar Mangalam Birla. Their views of what industry's constraints are will be heard, and should be because they have crores of rupees invested and can invest crores more. Or the large associations are invited—CII, Federation of Indian Chambers of Commerce and Industry (FICCI), and Assocham. Then their presidents, who are invariably CEOs of large companies, represent them.

The voices of the little fellows are hardly ever heard. Their problems are not the same as the big boys' problems. Some principal problems MSMEs face, which we learned in the prime minister's task force's consultations with them, are: obtaining finance at low cost, and the harassment of dealing with government functionaries and inspectors.

A healthy system

The World Bank's assessment of countries' business regulatory environments correctly tries to take the perspective of small enterprises. Therefore, it has the right focus. But there are problems in the design and execution of the process, which I learned when I was a Member of the Independent Panel that the president of the World Bank set up in 2012 to examine the World Bank's Doing Business report. Many countries, including China and India, had complained that the report was inaccurate and not useful because its methodology was flawed. The Panel was led by Mr Trevor Manuel, planning minister of South Africa. The Panel interviewed representatives of many countries' governments, also business associations, and labour unions, and several divisions of the World Bank itself, amongst whom there were disagreements about the report. The Panel discussed its findings with the authors of the report and understood their views and limitations too.

A principal weakness of the report is that it jumps to conclusions from very limited evidence. For example, it will assess the state of the business regulatory environment in a country by examining the conditions in one or two cities at the most in that country. The constraints that MSMEs in India face were, until recently, generalized by the World Bank from an examination of conditions in Mumbai. Now Delhi has been added as the second city. The World Bank has to manage its costs, so it cannot go to many cities. India has

MSMEs across the country and they must grow everywhere to create jobs and ensure inclusive development. The difficulties of doing business in Uttar Pradesh, Bengal, Punjab, or Odisha are different, and perhaps more than in Mumbai and Delhi. By easing the constraints on enterprises in Mumbai and Delhi, India may improve its ranking in the World Bank's evaluations. But it would not have any significant effect on the growth of the MSME sector in the country.

Another issue with the World Bank's Doing Business methodology is the type of information it considers to evaluate conditions for doing business. 'Objective' criteria are emphasized, and 'subjective' views are not considered. This can lead to erroneous assessments. For example, the one factor on which India does well in the World Bank's rankings is the availability of finance for enterprises. India ranks 25th on this factor, whereas India's overall ranking is 142. I found this surprising because in the extensive consultations done with MSMEs by the prime minister's Task Force, availability of finance was the biggest constraint. The World Bank's Doing Business team explained that India ranked high because the government had issued a guideline to banks that 60 per cent of the lending to the priority sector must go to MSMEs. The fact on the ground was that the actual levels were much less because there are implementation problems with this policy. Therefore, whatever the policies may say, the MSMEs must be asked what is actually happening. Such information has to be obtained from 'subjective' sources for the reality to be known.

If India wants to really improve the conditions for MSMEs, it cannot take short-cuts like the World Bank report does. The MSMEs must be consulted. And since MSMEs operate in all the states, and not just in two metro cities, and because conditions may not be the same in all states, assessments must be made in each state in consultation with MSMEs operating in the states.

Conceptual and ideological problems

The Independent Panel also noticed some conceptual problems with the World Bank's methodology. These were related principally to the assessment of tax regimes and labour laws in the countries. When the report was first introduced over ten years ago, countries with the lowest levels of taxes on enterprises ranked highest on the taxation score in the World Bank's ease of doing business index. There were objections to this from within the World Bank itself. Governments must have tax revenues to provide transportation and energy infrastructure, and education and social security systems that industrial enterprises expect governments to provide to make it easier for enterprises to operate. Governments may feel compelled to reduce taxes on industry to attract investments, but this reduces their capabilities to provide and maintain physical and social infrastructure. In the long run, industry also suffers.

In the early years of the World Bank's Doing Business report, while rating the quality of labour laws, high weightage was given to the ease with which labour could be fired. This approach was found to be wrong because industry also expects that there will be skilled people available for it to operate productively. Skill development requires investment from the industry itself and reasonable continuity of employment to enable skills to be improved. Industries like to operate in countries and regions in which there are harmonious industrial relations, for which industrial relations practices that create more harmony, fair treatment of employees, and good social security systems are also required.

Taxes are required and good industrial relations practices are required for the industry's own good. Labour laws and taxes are required for the benefit of other stakeholders in society too. Therefore, all stakeholders must be consulted while designing labour laws and tax systems. Consultation with stakeholders is required for regulations in other areas too, such as land use and environment impact laws. Laws in such matters should not be changed just to suit industry, whose demands may be short-sighted. No doubt deliberations amongst stakeholders can be contentious. But that is not a sufficient reason to avoid them. Better ways of conducting these deliberations must be applied to convert potential (and actual) contentions into collaboration. In that way the system can be improved for everyone.

Collaboration and coordination

Amongst the twenty-six working groups created during my efforts to bolster the manufacturing sector in India, one was to look into the business regulatory environment. Each of the working groups was chaired by a secretary of the government of India or by a senior industrialist. In view of its critical importance, the working group on the business regulatory environment was co-chaired by the Secretary of the Ministry of Corporate Affairs and myself. We examined the reports of others who had looked at India's business regulations. We looked at the experience of other countries. We developed an implementation plan.

Soon after this, Dr Veerappa Moily became the country's minister for corporate affairs. One of the first steps he took was to announce the formation of a committee to look into the business regulatory environment in India. He approached the deputy chairman of the Planning Commission to nominate a representative of the Planning Commission on this committee. The deputy chairman, Montek Ahluwalia, was surprised since there was already a plan which evidently Dr Moily did not know of. He asked me to speak to Dr Moily.

I told Dr Moily about the plan made by the working group,

and asked him why it was necessary to have yet another committee to go into the same subject. Would it not be better if everyone cooperated in implementing a plan already made? He was surprised to hear about the plan, which was ready. I told him his own ministry's secretary had been a co-chairman of the working group. Lack of coordination is often described as the left hand not knowing what the right hand is doing. Here was a case of the left hand not knowing what the left hand was doing!

Amongst the cartoons by R.K. Laxman that he kindly allowed me to use in my book *Remaking India: One Country, One Destiny* in 2004, there is one to illustratic this point. It shows a government minister angrily telling a bureaucrat, 'The problem of this village is still not solved? But we held debates and seminars on the problem. We must hold more seminars and discussions.' 'And appoint another committee!' I would add.

Whenever there is a need to address some issue, the instinct of ministers in the government is to appoint another committee. Even if many committees have already looked into the very same issue. So there are more committees and more reports and nothing much gets done while people are getting impatient for results. In this instance it is the MSMEs who have been waiting a long time for the government to get its act together. They want the business regulatory environment to be improved so that they can compete with the rest of the world with both their hands applied to improving their businesses rather than having one hand always required to deal with corruption and to fend off red tape.

India has an implementation problem. And the implementation problem in India is very often caused by contentions amongst stakeholders and confusion amongst agencies who should coordinate amongst themselves.

Many consulting organizations have been studying

the challenges faced by business enterprises in India and publishing reports about what the government should do to stimulate the growth of manufacturing in the country. All of them have concluded that two-thirds of the business regulatory issues that affect enterprises, especially small ones, are in the purview of state governments. Therefore, the question is, what should the central government do to improve business regulatory conditions in the country?

I summarize the challenges for improving the business regulatory environment.

1. The responsibility for making improvements is principally with the state governments.
2. Conditions in all the states are not the same so each state will have to make its own specific plan.
3. Several stakeholder groups in the state should be engaged to tune up the regulations. These must include industry, especially small industries. Other stakeholders representing labour, environment, and other interests must be included too.
4. Many government departments within the state must coordinate amongst themselves to make the improvements.
5. At the central government level, there are many organizations who have responsibilities for improving the business environment in the country including Department of Industrial Policy and Promotion (DIPP), the MSME Ministry and the Ministry of Corporate Affairs. The Planning Commission is one of these too. Turf issues amongst them is making coordination amongst them very difficult.
6. Many industrial development organizations, consulting companies, and business associations have useful capabilities and are willing to support

the central and state governments.

7. If India has to become a more attractive place than other countries for investments in industry, then India must improve the business regulatory environment *faster than other countries are improving their business regulatory environments.*

8. Therefore, India must focus on improving coordination within the states and in the centre, and also collaboration amongst stakeholders *much faster than other countries are improving their processes for collaboration and coordination.* If India does not do this, India will not be able to move up the rankings of countries for real ease of doing business. The shortcut to improving India's rankings is to fix conditions only in the two cities in India that the World Bank surveys. However, this will not enable enterprises to grow around India, which must be the objective of India's manufacturing strategy.

Despite their concerns and best intentions, the many stakeholders were unable to satisfactorily reach their common objective of improving the business regulatory environment because of poor coordination amongst themselves. There was no platform on which the state governments, who should be the principal actors to bring about the changes, could interact to share their experiences and learn from each other. Neither was there a process through which organizations that had knowledge of good practices, such as international development agencies and consulting organizations, could impart such knowledge to the state governments. The central government agencies, such as the Planning Commission and central government ministries, were more involved in allocation of funds rather than enabling states to learn from each other.

A process had to be constructed to bring the many stakeholders and enablers together, to systematically align their efforts, and thus speed up the improvement of the business regulatory environment. A core idea adopted by the Total Quality movement, the learning cycle, proved very useful for this. The learning cycle is a process of learning in action: of stretching towards a goal; experimenting with a new way to reach it; reflecting on the results and making a better hypothesis to guide the next thrust (the next experiment); then reflecting on that one, and improving; and so on.

The Learning Cycle

Activities required to accelerate a national learning cycle in India to improve the business regulatory environment faster were mapped onto the model of a learning cycle, as shown in the diagram.

The first step is to motivate the states to make improvements. The World Bank's low rating of India as a country has spurred the central government. The Indian states could be further spurred on by a comparison amongst Indian states. They could compete with each other to attract investments. India's low rankings compared to countries like Singapore and Finland, and many other countries ahead of India in the World Bank's rankings, can be explained away by pointing out that conditions in such countries are very different to India. On the other hand, Indian states operate under the same constitutional laws and in similar conditions. Therefore, if an Indian state can get ahead of others, there would be something that other Indian states could learn and apply. States who have been spurred on to improve can learn good practices from other states. Such processes can be shared by a combination of methods—online and face-to-face. A useful 'knowledge management' system can construct and manage these processes.

It is not enough to merely know a best practice. It has to be applied to produce a result. A memorable encounter between a consulting organization and an Indian policymaker was the presentation by one of the world's largest strategy consulting firms to a former prime minister of India, Atal Bihari Vajpayee. They presented to him the nine things that must be done to increase India's GDP growth to 9 per cent per annum. He listened patiently and then observed: 'We know all this. The question is: how will it be done?' His point was, how are changes in policies to be implemented in a large, democratic country, with stakeholders pulling in many directions?

Application of an idea in a democratic system with multiple stakeholders is not easy, as Prime Minister Vajpayee had observed. Good processes for creating cooperation amongst stakeholders and coordination of their actions will enable faster implementation. Here, IbIn-like processes are very useful, and they should be adopted by the states.

The fourth step in the learning cycle is the comparison of the states in the next year. This time, it is not who is at the top that would be most interesting, but *who made the most improvement.* Then, this winner's methods for making the changes can be analysed. And best practices for implementation in multi-stakeholder systems (and within the Indian context too) can be distilled and shared in the next cycle.

The Planning Commission took the first step in 2013. It developed an evaluation framework for Indian states, for assessing those matters that affect enterprises, especially small ones, and in the states. Useful ideas from the World Bank's methodology for evaluating ease of doing business across countries were adopted too. The comparison of the states was published by the Planning Commission in early 2014. It did not publicize the results widely then because the

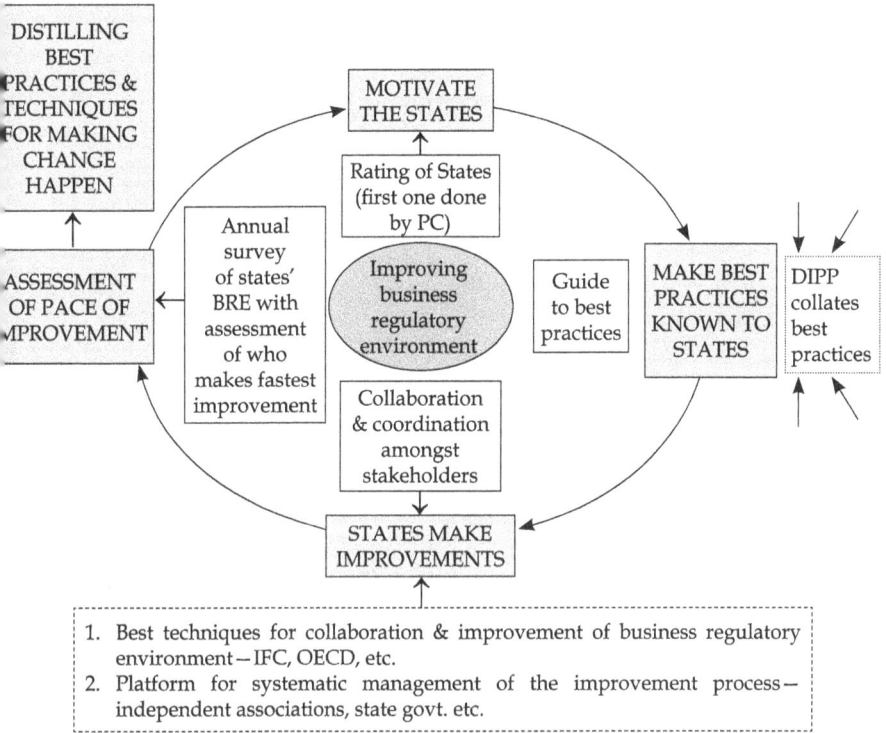

Figure 5: The national learning cycle.

national elections were underway and the code of conduct was in play regarding statements by the government that could influence voter preferences. However, the evaluation framework is available and another round of comparisons should be done now. The other steps in the learning cycle have to also be induced for learning and implementation to be accelerated in the states. The NITI Aayog has been charged with processes for promoting collaborative and competitive federalism. Therefore, it could be the facilitator of the learning cycle.

FOUR

BUILDING BRIDGES FOR TRUST

For one hundred million additional jobs to be created in the next decade, to engage Indian youth coming of employment age, constraints on the growth of enterprises, especially small ones, must be removed. Amongst the major constraints, which include inadequate transportation and energy infrastructure and the dysfunctional business regulatory environment, are human resource related issues. These issues include shortage of adequately skilled workers, shortage of good manufacturing managers (with the swing of engineers to IT jobs in the past fifteen years), deteriorating industrial relations (IR), and a need to reform labour laws.

In 2012, when I was a member of the Planning Commission, Dr Surinder Kapur, chairman of CII (the Confederation of Indian Industry)'s Industrial Relations Committee, asked me for help. As chairman of the committee, Surinder wanted the members of CII to understand that India would not grow its manufacturing sector if owners and managers of enterprises did not value their workmen. He was having some difficulty in persuading them and wanted my support.

The subject of 'Industrial Relations', that is, relations with blue collar workers, has been coming back on the agenda of top managements in India recently. With the rise of the more glamorous Indian IT industry from the late 1990s, the management of human resources had become a white collar affair. Graduates of the Indian Institutes of Technology who would have earlier gone to manufacturing companies, were now flocking to IT companies. Also, since India had become the global hotspot for BPO companies, they too were hiring young people in large numbers. Indian IT and BPO companies made lots of money through labour cost arbitrage. The faster these companies could hire and train people, the faster they would make money for their investors. Human resource management was perhaps the most critical function in these companies. The best practices of these white collar companies were reported in the media. The development, management, and retention of blue collar workers became a much less glamorous subject, and it seemed to hardly receive any attention of the top corporate managers.

Dr Surinder Kapur is an outstanding manager of industrial relations. The firebrand union leader, Datta Samant, who had brought the entire textile industry in Mumbai to its knees in the 1970s and caused it to collapse, had also organized the workers in Surinder's company, Bharat Gears. However, industrial relations in Surinder's company remained harmonious and his company prospered. Later, Surinder founded Sona Steering, which won the international Deming Prize for quality. Thereafter he bought an ailing manufacturing company in Germany, and turned it around with the cooperation of German unions.

Surinder Kapur and I became friends in the early 1980s when he was the CEO of Bharat Gears, and I was the resident director of the Tata Engineering and Locomotive Company in Pune, to whom his company supplied gear parts. One day we ran into each other in the book shop in the Taj Mahal Hotel in Mumbai. There, standing amongst the book shelves, each with a book in hand, we decided the time had come for Indian auto parts producers to sell to US auto original equipment manufacturers (OEMs)! We set out on an exploratory mission to the US a few days later and returned with drawings and requests to bid from the three large OEMs—GM, Ford, and Chrysler.

On our return, Surinder invited me to speak to the national council of the Automobile Component Manufacturers Association (ACMA) about new global opportunities for Indian auto parts producers. The council members were sceptical. They said that Indian manufacturers did not have the quality standards to compete with Japanese and Korean parts producers to sell to American OEMs. But some seeds of ambition were sown. Some Indian auto parts companies embarked on drives to improve their manufacturing quality and productivity. Over the next fifteen years, the largest numbers of winners outside Japan, of the Deming Quality Medal, the highest prize for quality in the world perhaps, were Indian auto parts producers! Not only did they win prizes, they successfully won orders in the US, Europe, and even Japan, and made large profits in the process too.

The essence of the Total Quality Movement is engagement of workers, especially blue collar workers, to improve production processes. Workers who operate machines and assemble products have the most intimate knowledge of the processes. When these workers are provided quality management tools, time, and encouragement, they will improve the productivity of the machines and materials they handle. Such bottom-up improvements by workers can add up to very large productivity gains for a company. That is how Japanese companies had transformed themselves by the 1980s, from mere low cost producers to world beaters in many manufacturing industries, including automobiles, white goods, and entertainment products.

When American companies realized that the secret weapon of the Japanese companies was TQM, they too began to introduce it into their factories. Many American companies hired Professor Joseph M. Juran to advise them. Professor Juran was one of the two American gurus who had introduced new ideas of TQM to Japan after the Second World War; the other was Professor Deming. It took American managers quite some time to realize that the power of TQM lay in the respect Japanese managers gave to their workers and the development of their workers' capabilities. I was consulting to the American OEMs myself at that time. I vividly recall an interview that the PBS TV channel broadcasted with Professor Juran. The interviewer asked him whether the American companies would catch up with the Japanese now that they were adopting TQM too. Professor Juran seemed to have tears in his eyes when he said: 'They don't get it. It's not the maths and machines. It is the people they should pay attention to! The people make the difference.'

The 'appreciating assets' of an enterprise

An 'ideological' contention, between industry leaders, had become visible in the course of the development of the plan to grow India's manufacturing sector. For many, the difficulty of firing labour at will was a big problem in improving productivity and a deterrent to growth of their industry. For some, however, the problems they were focused on were: how to develop more skills within their enterprises; how to improve the quality of relationships within them; and how to retain the talent they nurtured. One view was that workers are a problem and worker-related costs must be minimized at all times. The other view was that workers (and human resources generally) are the real assets of the enterprise, and the source of its ability to improve productivity and competitiveness.

The Planning Commission decided to test these two theories by comparing the topline and profit performances of companies with different approaches to their human resources.

Bain and Company undertook this study. It compared companies within the same industries, and often in the same states in India. Thus the companies being compared were subject to the same labour laws and regulations. The study showed conclusively that those companies that considered their employees as their 'appreciating assets' out-performed those who took a more mechanical, legal, and predominantly cost-driven approach to their employees. This report stirred a lot of reflection within industry.

Historically, industrialization has been the process by which countries have grown their economies and become more 'developed' than others. Industrialization is a process of producing new items that were not produced before. Advanced industrialization is the development and production of even more sophisticated items by enterprises in the country. Thus, industrialization is a process of learning to do what could not be done before, and learning to produce what could not be produced before. Industrial nations are overtaken by later industrializing nations if enterprises in the rising nations learn to perform better than the established leaders. Thus, Japanese producers in many industries — automobiles, electronics, steel, chemicals, machinery, and others — overtook much larger American and European companies, and became very large themselves. Korea followed, and some of its companies caught up and overtook even the Japanese companies.

Enterprises within countries and amongst countries compete with their abilities to produce things that others cannot, or to produce the same things better than others can. To compete with others, enterprises must learn faster than them.

Small companies grow when they are more competitive than larger ones, and overtake them. Size at the starting line is not an indicator of who wins the race: the ability of the company, large or small, to learn faster than others is the source of sustainable competitive advantage, within a country and globally as well.

The only resource in an enterprise that can learn and improve its own ability is the people in it. The value of all other resources — machines, buildings, and materials, will depreciate with time, but the value of the people can appreciate as they learn to do things they could not do before, and learn to do them better. Therefore, the only 'appreciating assets' in the enterprise are its people. They are the source of its sustainable competitive advantage, provided they are motivated to learn and enabled to learn faster by the conditions in the enterprise. This insight has great implications for India's strategy to grow its manufacturing sector. India has an abundance of people seeking jobs. They can provide a long-term competitive advantage to enterprises in India — provided they are treated as the appreciating assets of enterprises.

Market economists say that labour 'markets' in India must be improved. They complain that 'rigidities' are stifling the country's labour markets. They say that transaction costs must be low and it should be possible to conclude transactions quickly and easily to improve the quality of a market. They are right. 'Online markets' are expanding because they enable quick transactions with very low transaction costs. However, for markets to grow, one must not have only low transaction costs. There must be more to sell and there must be more buyers too. In labour markets, there must be jobs to sell and people with skills to buy the jobs who must be brought together.

While in a market buyers and sellers are on separate sides of the market, such as sellers and buyers of homes and sellers and buyers of automobiles (who are brought together in the market), a labour market is different. In a labour market, the supply side and demand side cannot be separated so easily. They cannot be separated because the development of skills requires people to learn and improve their skills by doing jobs. At the same time, application of skills within enterprises improves the productivity of enterprises and their competitiveness, and this creates more jobs. Some part of the skill development, the more elementary parts, can be done offline. But the honing of skills, which makes organizations more productive and more competitive, can happen only on the job.

Therefore, to develop a strong labour market in India, owners and managers of manufacturing enterprises will have to change their relationships with their employees. They must realize that their employees are their 'appreciating assets'.

The stuck record

Around the same time that Surinder Kapur approached me to support his agenda as chairman of CII's National Industrial Relations' Committee, Rajeev Dubey, president of the Employers' Federation of India, also approached me. He was organizing many seminars to get employers to understand the benefits of harmonious industrial relations.

Both Rajeev and Surinder had invited union leaders for some of their meetings and felt that there was a possibility of cooperation amongst unions and industry associations to improve the industrial relations climate in the country. They suggested I invite a few union leaders along with some leaders of industry associations to an informal meeting in the Planning Commission. Thus a dialogue could begin on how, together, unions and employers could facilitate the growth of the Indian manufacturing industry.

A year earlier, Dr Kavita Gupta, Principal Secretary (Labour) in the Maharashtra government had requested me to assist her to improve industrial relations in the state. She wanted to invite the leaders of all principal unions and all principal employers' federations to a meeting and she felt my presence would be an inducement for them to come. As it turned out, she had a full house: all the unions and all the industry associations showed up.

The meeting began with both sides stating their positions and suggesting the other side was the problem. I asked the industry leaders how often they had said the same things to the unions in the past. The reply was that they had been saying this for the past fifteen to twenty years but the unions would not get it. When asked the same question, the union leaders said they, too, had been repeating what they had said for a long time, but the employers would not listen. Both sides have been repeating their views for a long time without the other side listening! Both sides viewed each other as a problem. When they met they talked 'at' each other, whereas what was required was to talk 'with' each other.

It became clear that the format of the discussion between unions and employees would have to change for the gramophone needle in the cracked record to become unstuck. For solutions to be found, there would have to be more listening to the other, rather than repeating one's own position again and again. There must be a willingness to acknowledge at least some truth in the other's perspective and thus make space for one's own perspective to be acknowledged. More trust in each other must be developed so that solutions can be co-created.

Both sides agreed that the labour market must be 'fair and flexible'. Unions said that they wanted employers to have flexibility. They wanted industries to grow so that employment would grow. They understood very well that unless Indian industries were competitive with industries in China and other countries, they would not grow. They acknowledged that businesses had ups and downs and, therefore, employers must have the flexibility to adjust the numbers of their employees. However, they insisted that there must always be fairness in dealing with the employees.

A pernicious practice that had crept into Indian industry was the engagement of labour through contractors rather than as regular employees of the enterprise. Employers said they had to resort to this practice to have the flexibility they needed, which the rigid labour laws denied them. The study of labour practices that Bain had done for the Planning Commission had revealed some startling facts. In almost all Indian companies in almost all industries, very large numbers of contractor workers were being employed—ranging from over 50 per cent to 80 per cent. Moreover, the majority of these workers were doing regular production jobs, not incidental service jobs.

This startlingly large number makes one question an oft-repeated statement by some economists that Indian companies have been loath to employ more people because of rigid labour laws, and have been investing in capital equipment instead. The evidence is that they have been employing more workers. However, the workers are being employed through contractors, which gives employers flexibility to adjust the sizes of their workforces. The levels of contract employment—from over 50 per cent to 80 per cent—is startling because they greatly exceed the levels of flexibility the companies need. Fluctuations in production are hardly that large in any industry.

Since these large numbers of workers are not being paid the wages that regular employees get for doing the same work, there is gross unfairness. An explanation from industry, though it cannot justify the unfairness, is that industry's costs will become too high if the contract workers were to be paid as well as regular employees in the companies. The Bain team did some calculations with information that some companies gave them. They found that if the contract workers were paid at least at the lowest level that a permanent employee was paid, there would be little impact on the profits of the companies. The reason is that total employee costs in companies in the manufacturing sector in India, which include compensations to their CEOs and senior executives, are less than 10 per cent of all costs. Contract labour costs are a fraction of these. Increase them, even quite a bit, and the effect on the companies' profits is small. In fact, Bain found that the reduction may be less than 5 per cent of the profits.

These numbers seemed unbelievable to the companies. They cross-checked them. The numbers were not wrong. What some companies found when they looked into their industrial relations practices dismayed them. They found that contract workers were not being provided canteen facilities so that they could eat in dignity. They were not even provided safety equipment. It seems Indian labour markets were performing. They were giving employers the flexibility they wanted (and more) and also at low cost. But the way the labour market was functioning to make it easy for employers to adjust workforce sizes and costs was not good. It was creating inequities. Even the employers said there should be fairness along with flexibility.

Some large companies in the Western region were dismayed when these facts came to light. The bad practices had developed unknown to their top management, it seems. These companies began to remove the inequities. And others have begun to follow them.

A new initiative

The need to reform labour laws has been acknowledged by all stakeholders: the unions, industry, and government. The laws, they say, are too many, antiquated, and badly administered in general. Demands to reform labour laws have been made for twenty-five years by both industry and unions and several attempts to reform them have been made by the government, but there has been little progress so far. The system is trapped in the rut mentioned before: you cannot keep using the same process that has contributed to the problem and expect a different outcome.

I was often accused by economists in the Planning Commission (and outside it too) of being anti-labour law reform, though I was not. I was a strong advocate of reforming the antiquated and badly administered laws, but I was advocating another approach to improve the labour laws. My view was that we must first find out what improvements are required in the quality of industrial relations, and what changes in laws would be necessary to enable these improvements. For this, the stakeholders must be involved, namely, employers and representatives of employees. The stakeholders' involvement is required in determining what changes are required because their support is necessary for the implementation of the changes, in the practices and the laws. We must change the laws, I said. However, we must change the way we are going about trying to change the laws. The process being followed so far had become too antagonistic and too legalistic, I said. There was too little meeting of minds and hearts amongst the stakeholders.

The labour law issues that must be addressed relate to terms of employment (including contract labour and termination issues), payment of wages (equity, amount, and mode of payment), safety, and social benefits (especially to the unorganized sector), right to representation, and apprenticeship. There is contention amongst the stakeholders about how these subjects should be tackled and what should be the changes in laws and regulations.

At their first meeting together in the Planning Commission, the union and management leaders recounted their disappointments with the official tripartite processes.

Agreements seemed to have been reached — at least according to the records. But they were not implemented. And so another round of discussions would follow, but that too would turn out to be a formality with no results afterwards. Therefore, both unions and managements agreed that it is the process of deliberation that must be changed to get better results.

Important decisions regarding the design of the dialogue process between unions and employers were taken early on. One decision was to invite some leaders of industry federations and some leaders from the union side and to invite them to come in their personal capacity, though they are designated leaders within their organizations. The leaders invited would be persons willing to step out of the 'stuck record' of discourse so far, and willing to listen to opposing views because they cared very much to produce better relationships between stakeholders rather than to win the argument for their side. Though the leaders would be persons who carried weight within 'their side', they would not be expected to automatically commit their organizations to new ideas that emerged in the dialogue. They would go back to their organizations and get wider support for them.

The intention of the dialogue, it was agreed, would be to build new bridges across the divides between the stakeholder groups even before all internal divides within the groups could be resolved. The emergence of new possibilities, created by leaders from both sides working together in a new dialogue, would inspire 'fence sitters' within the stakeholder groups to come along, and thus a movement of change would 'snow ball'. It was accepted that there may be permanent nay-sayers on both sides, but they would matter less when the movement for change had become stronger.

The IbIn team facilitated the growth of the consensus by urging representatives from national unions and employers' associations to come together in a new dialogue. The objective of this process is to provide the stakeholders another platform, outside the formal systems of tripartite labour conferences. On this platform they could hear each other in a new way and together develop solutions that will ensure that the rights of employees are respected, while also creating conditions that will allow employers to improve the competitiveness of their enterprises and thus grow them faster (thereby creating more employment too).

The dialogue between the stakeholders steadily deepened and grew. Very early on, the participants agreed that they would pay as much attention to the quality of their interactions as they would to the content of their discussions. They realized that the process is the means with which they can produce the outcome they want. If the process is not good, the outcome is unlikely to come about. To use another metaphor, the process was a bridge over which they would cross together. If the bridge was too weak to take the burden of their contentions, it would collapse, and their dialogue would fail to reach its desired ends. Therefore, they must pay attention to the bridge, which could also be referred to as the 'platform' for their interactions. The words 'process' and 'platform' became interchangeable in their lexicon. Both referred to the bridge they were building and using at the same time for their deliberations about the contentious issues that must be resolved.

The two-tracked process, of patiently building the bridge while impatiently wishing to find concrete solutions to long-standing issues, proves a challenge in any project of creating a new platform or process for stakeholders to work together. The need to solve big problems, which have not been solved by other means, entices them to try the new process offered. They want the process to produce results fast to prove it works or they abandon it. In their impatience to find solutions, they persist with the behaviours they are familiar with and do not appreciate that it is their behaviours in the meetings that they must focus on and change if they want to find solutions now. Thus they overload the bridge too soon and it breaks. Therefore, the progress of the project must be assessed by both, the progress being made in building a new and strong bridge, and progress in resolving the contentious issues. Progress in resolving issues cannot get ahead of the bridge-building.

The participants in the IR dialogue have understood this. The bridge is the trust between them, which they have observed strengthening in each meeting. In fact, the building of trust has become a principal objective. Trust in each other increased when they became aware of their own habitual thoughts and behaviours towards each other that they had to change to have a new possibility of finding solutions that they have not been able to with their traditional forms of debates. By concentrating on the quality of the trust, they are paying as much attention to the bridge as to the material (the content of the discussion) they are moving across it.

Learning in action

The IbIn team assisted the leaders of the employers' associations and unions to together build their bridge (or their 'platform' or their 'process', which are other inter-changeable terms they have used to refer to the bridge).

Often the participants revert into an old-time, old-style argument. Old wounds do not heal easily, and old habits die hard. Whenever they surface, someone in the group will remind everyone about why they have come together and what they want to accomplish together. The shared vision of better, more trusting industrial relations to achieve the national objective of more jobs, and better jobs, and more competitive enterprises, draws them out of their old rutted debates very quickly. This is the magnetic power of a shared vision, which they draw upon.

Whenever new members come into the process, as many more are, it is necessary to make them a part of the vision community. Therefore, the shared vision is recalled for them and they buy into it too. Thereafter it is their magnet as well. It can pull them out of their entrenched behaviour patterns whenever they must rise above their squabbles to work with each other towards the shared vision.

An insight the IbIn team had, which they have shared with the participants of the industrial relations dialogue between the unions and employers, is that their platform rests on three legs, like a tripod. To raise their platform and make it more stable, the three legs must be made stronger, and must grow together. The three legs of the process are:

1. Build trust
2. Take ownership
3. Apply a systematic approach in the dialogue

The participants must take ownership of the process themselves. It is their process to obtain ends they want. A systematic process is essential, otherwise the dialogue will break down. Trust is the key. It will be low in the beginning, as it was amongst the participants in the industrial relations dialogue. Old histories, ingrained impressions of others, and rehearsed actions and reactions that are habitually repeated make it very difficult to get out of the deep rut into which the debates have settled and to find new solutions. Thus, mistrust results in more mistrust. To get the needle out of the stuck record, the co-owners of the process must make increase in trust in each other an objective of the process, and for this they must apply good principles in the conduct of their process. Then they will increase trust in each other and find new solutions together.

FIVE

DELIVERING CHANGE

With a daily circulation of 1.5 million, the Sakal Marathi newspaper is amongst the top ten regional language newspapers in the country. In 2012 Sakal, a Maharashtra-based group, organized a movement in the city of Pune in an unusual way to promote the use of public transport. Because seeing is believing and believing leads to committing, Sakal decided that Pune's citizens should actually experience a vision of their city with much more public transport and correspondingly, less need for private transport vehicles. The intention was to generate stronger public commitment and pressure to provide more public transport in the city.

Thus 'Pune Bus Day' was conceived for their purpose. A plan was made with participation of diverse groups of citizens: several civil society organizations, industry chambers, traders' associations, and government departments, to provide and run sufficient buses on one day so that citizens would not need to use private transportation that day. Accordingly, money was raised to hire more buses from other cities, routes for their deployment in Pune were planned, route maps were circulated through schools and colleges and public enthusiasm was created by the newspaper for the day-long experiment. The passionate involvement of citizens is epitomized by pictures of housewives who volunteered to wash and clean the buses before they were deployed so that a common complaint of citizens about public transport, its uncleanness, was addressed!

The Pune Bus Day was a great success. Most owners of private transport cooperated and travelled by bus on that day. Measurements revealed that pollution levels in the city were substantially reduced, as were the numbers of road accidents. Thus, the benefits of the vision were made real.

The challenge thereafter was to make an ad hoc experiment into a permanent reality. For this, more buses would have to be bought by the municipal transport corporation, staff hired and trained and their salaries provided for, permanent bus shelters installed, and so on. These changes require the power and the resources of government machinery, the movement of which requires inter-departmental coordination, and implementation of an overall plan that is adopted by all wings of the government, at the city and state levels. The need to address this challenge of aligning government power with people's passion drew the Sakal Group to the mission of IbIn, which is to propagate systematic methods for converting contentions amongst stakeholders into collaboration, and confusion amongst agencies into coordination, so that plans can be implemented, and desired outcomes produced.

IbIn, with the help of the World Bank, introduced the Sakal Group to Pemandu, the delivery unit created in the Malaysian prime minister's office to develop plans made by collaboration amongst stakeholders in Malaysia to produce desired outcomes in a time-bound manner. Pemandu had the 'technology' that Sakal was looking for to systematically engage government agencies and experts with the planning and implementation of public missions. Sakal and Pemandu entered into an agreement to make the Pemandu methodology available in India through the Sakal Foundation.

An essential requirement for the application of the Pemandu methodology, which entails intensive involvement of government agencies, is sponsorship of the process by top levels of government so that government officers (and senior persons from the private sector, and experts too) are motivated to participate in the process. Therefore, the Sakal Foundation offered the Pemandu methodology to the chief minister and the government of Maharashtra for making and implementing plans for the state of Maharashtra.

An innovation that Sakal introduced to the Pemandu methodology was systematic participation of citizens to select the areas in which they wanted better results. This was achieved by the engagement of women in Maharashtra through the Tanishka movement that the Sakal Foundation runs. Tanishka engages with hundreds of women self-help groups throughout Maharashtra.

A consultation was organized by Sakal through the women self-help groups to determine citizens' priorities. Water-related issues emerged as the topmost priority. Maharashtra is afflicted with acute water problems: large parts of the state are drought-prone leading even to distressing farmer suicides, and other parts suffer from periodic floods. Many segments of society are concerned with water-related problems: agriculture, industry, and consumers in rural and urban areas. Therefore, a plan to alleviate the state's water problems requires that many stakeholders' needs must be considered – and they are often in contention – and that systemic solutions be found and implemented rather than quick-fixes to alleviate one set of concerns that cause other problems.

The state government accepted that water should be the issue to which the Pemandu–Sakal methodology would be applied.

The heart of the Pemandu methodology is a 'lab process' to create convergent plans. As a first step, in a 'pre-lab' process, data regarding the issue is gathered and analysed to determine the extent of the problem and its likely origins. This is a conventional step of problem diagnosis. However, the next step of the Pemandu process is the unusual one. Stakeholders relevant to the issue at hand are selected from the government, the private sector, and civil society, and they are required to work together for a few weeks, in a time-bound manner, and to use the systematic Pemandu methodology to convert the intentions of the plan (in this case to 'make Maharashtra drought-free in five years') into the steps that must be taken on the ground by various actors in a coordinated manner to achieve the desired result. Thus, a top-down, 30,000 foot intention is converted into 3-foot level actions.

The Pemandu methodology requires that the 3-foot level plans are produced by the implementing agencies themselves, working in unison with other agencies who make their 3-foot plans simultaneously within the same short period. This approach is different to conventional approaches of planning in which plans are made remotely by experts and others in authority, and then passed on for execution to the implementers who do not 'buy into' these plans, and often find that the plans are out of touch with ground realities.

After the plans are made in a participative manner, the sponsoring authority ensures that they are implemented. For this, a 'programme management unit' is set up that uses a programme management methodology to keep the sponsor informed of progress. Also, this unit alerts the implementers themselves about slippages so that they can take corrective actions. This unit, with the support of the sponsors' authority where required, tries to remove the bottlenecks in implementation. Ultimately, the sponsoring authority itself — in the Malaysian case, the prime minister — can intervene with the defaulting ministry or agency following the performance reviews. Thus, implementation is managed in a systematic manner.

Methods for 'convergent planning', which is the purpose

of the Pemandu 'labs', are used by strategy consulting companies for their clients all over the world. Indeed, the Pemandu 'labs' were developed and introduced in Malaysia by international consulting companies. Such methodologies fit well into situations with an empowered 'CEO' who can enforce the plan, as there generally is in the corporate sector. However, in the public governance sphere, especially wherever democratic participation is an applied norm, people's support for the intentions of the plan becomes essential to ensure that it will be implementable. Experience has shown that people's support is not easy to obtain with mere data and analysis. An 'emotional connect' is essential to win the people's support.

The importance of an emotional connect with people in any substantial government-led transformation process has been endorsed in examinations of large-scale reform programmes in democracies in South America and Southeast Asia, which were recently conducted by the Global Economic Symposium and by the World Bank. (In fact, the importance of an emotional connect with the public, and the processes for obtaining it, such as the Tanishka programme of Sakal, have been appreciated by Pemandu of Malaysia and will henceforth be incorporated by Pemandu also.) Therefore, an integral part of any process to make plans in a plural democracy must be systematic methods for connecting with citizens. India, with its history of non-violent citizens' engagement with political and social transformation inspired by Mahatma Gandhi, is a rich source for insights into methods of emotionally engaging citizens in large-scale reforms. IbIn has undertaken the distillation of best methods for this, in the Indian context at least, in another project, the 'CSO (Civil Society Organizations) initiative' supported by UNDP.

Another significant difference that was observed in the power structure of the executive, between Malaysia and India, though both are democracies, is in the relative stability of the government in power in Malaysia and the concentration of power within it. In the state of Maharashtra, into which the Pemandu methodology was first applied in India, there was a noisy coalition government in which the chief minister could not assert his authority like the prime minister in Malaysia could in his party, which had a large majority in Parliament and a long history of a very large majority. Moreover, with elections announced and a change in government expected in Maharashtra, the power of the chief minister as 'CEO' to lead a large-scale programme through implementation was clearly doubtful. Therefore, forces other than the authority of the CEO were required to obtain political alignment and continuity of political support for the plan. These forces can arise from public pressure on the political establishment. For this, the 'people connect' mentioned before is essential, and it can be amplified by the media.

Therefore, a public campaign in the media to publicize the demand for the plan and the progress of its implementation becomes the third essential component of a transformative planning and implementation process. In Maharashtra, the Sakal Group of newspapers provided a media platform for 'public pressure'. The combination of the 'people connect' through the women's organizations and the 'public pressure' through the media has forced a 'political alignment' as an outcome in Maharashtra. With this, the planning process for 'Water for All' was supported by all parties in the state's coalition government before the elections, and it continues to be supported (in fact even more strongly) by the newly elected government.

The three processes essential for a large, systemic change process in the public sector are described in the following diagram: People Connect, Public Pressure, and Convergent Planning. Political Alignment, as explained already, is an outcome principally of the People Connect and Public Pressure processes supported by Convergent Planning.

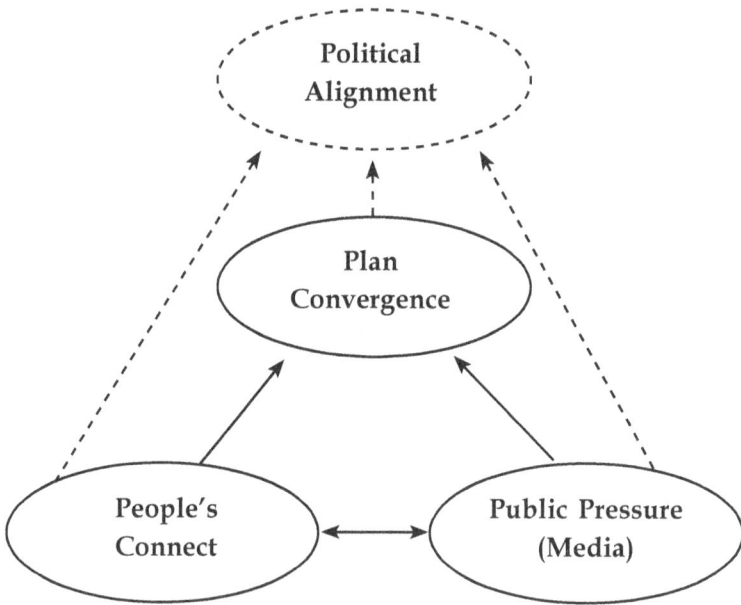

Figure 6: Alignment to public goals.

Two points need to be made about these processes. One is that there are principles and learnable methods for systematically managing Convergent Planning, People Connect, and Public Pressure processes. Indeed, as mentioned before, IbIn's objective was to look out for these.

The other point, about the process of connecting with local publics, is the necessity to use locally established and trusted channels—local civil society organizations and local media. Principles and methods are transportable across geographies: the trust in specific institutions is not.

Spreading around the application of systematic methods

The Sakal Group has created a foundation, the Delivering Change Foundation, to provide the support that the central government and Indian state governments are now asking for, seeing the good progress made by the application of new methodologies in the 'Water for All' programme in Maharashtra. The prime minister of India has publicly announced the intention to use the methodology more widely in the country. The new government in Maharashtra has signed a memorandum of understanding with the Delivering Change Foundation to set up a 'project management office' to oversee the implementation of the plans for the water sector that have been developed by the Labs, and also to extend the Lab process to develop plans for other sectors in the state.

Capacity must now be built within the country to meet the demands arising. The capacity-building process will have to ride along with work on new areas in the state and in the centre. Capacity development for 'soft skills' required for facilitation of complex processes requires that 'trainees' work on real-life situations to complete the capacity-building process. Concepts can be taught off-line, and some skills can be developed in simulated situations, but mastery of the skills requires application in real situations, albeit under the tutelage of coaches. A structured process, to induct potential facilitators, impart the training required (through classroom sessions, simulated training, and on-line coaching) is being designed by the Delivering Change Foundation.

The chief minister of Rajasthan, Ms Vasundhara Raje, is determined to deliver results to the state's citizens. She engaged an international consulting firm to set up a programme management office for her, and she is consulting with the firm to develop programmes for delivering change. The firm's methodology follows similar principles to the Pemandu–Sakal methodology, though it uses its own terminologies.

Recently, the state of Madhya Pradesh approached IbIn. A senior official of the state had participated in the IbIn workshop on 'simple systems of effective participative planning' in villages, in which one of the cases presented was the work being done in Maharashtra by the Delivering Change Foundation (DCF). The state's chief minister and she were keen to organize a conclave of stakeholders in the state to consider the adoption of methods such as the Pemandu–Sakal methodology for participative planning and implementation in the state. She wanted assistance to bring the Delivering Change Foundation and other consultants to this conclave. The states of Andhra Pradesh and Tamil Nadu have also begun to explore the application of these methods to accelerate the development of their states.

Like TQM did in Japan, IbIn methods are beginning to infect India. Sakal found Pemandu through the IbIn network and formed the Delivering Change Foundation. Subsequently, the state of Madhya Pradesh sought connections with DCF and other consulting firms who offered similar methods (albeit in competing versions) to choose whichever would be best for it. A 'market' of buyers and suppliers is forming for systematic methods for participative planning and implementation. The starting node of the network, the small start-up IbIn team, has planted some viable seeds.

The Planning Commission, in which IbIn was given birth, was closed sine die by the prime minister of India on 15 August 2014. A new body, the NITI Aayog, was formed in its place on 1 January 2015.

During the gap of many months between the closure of the Planning Commission and the opening of the NITI Aayog, the IbIn start-up team was housed in its 'dug-out' — its room without any partitions — provided to it by India@75 in Gurgaon. There it continued the search for, and the spreading around of, methods for systematic collaboration and participative planning.

The Planning Commission had been confused about whether it should be catalysing the adoption of better processes for collaboration and planning; NITI Aayog's charter requires it to do this. It must promote processes for 'cooperative federalism'; for stakeholders to come together systematically; and for participative planning.

The NITI Aayog is here. The start-up team's work is done.

SIX

RUSTING AND RESISTING CHANGE

I was preparing to join the government to serve the country when I finished my master's programme in physics in 1964. My life took a turn when I was persuaded by the directors of the Tata group that I could serve the country very well by joining the Tata Administrative Service instead of the Indian Administrative Service. After I turned sixty-five, I decided to 'hang up my boots' and put on a pair of golf shoes at last. Though I was not ready to go out to pasture, I thought I would have time now to get onto the greens and kill some time. Then, as mentioned earlier, while I was riding in a tram in Prague at the very beginning of a long promised holiday with my wife, I got a call from the prime minister of India. He invited me to join the government and serve the country as a member of the Planning Commission. I did not hesitate in accepting the invitation.

I had to scramble, and go through many anxious moments, to renounce my US citizenship and acquire my Indian citizenship again, so that I could take the oath to serve the Constitution and the people of India. I was asked to renounce all my formal associations outside the government so that I would have no conflicts of interest: the company boards I served on and the NGOs I chaired or served as a trustee of.

Now that I am no longer with the Planning Commission (and the government), many people ask me, was it worth it? My unhesitating answer is: Yes, every minute of it. The Planning Commission was the cockpit of the country's aeroplane. I had been perched in it behind the pilot—the prime minister. From the cockpit one could see the entire country. The chief ministers of all the states would come to the Planning Commission every year to explain how their states were doing and what their challenges were. The central ministries would be asked to explain how the country was doing in the subjects assigned to them: health, education, agriculture, industry, and others. Civil society organizations, industry associations, international development organizations, and many individuals, too, who had concerns and suggestions about the state of affairs in the country would come to the Planning Commission.

One could not get such a broad perspective from anywhere else. Furthermore, through the systematic engagement of citizen groups, business associations, labour unions, and many think-tanks in the process of developing the scenarios of India, that I have described earlier, I could get insights that could not be obtained merely by looking at statistics and reading voluminous reports about the country.

Most people who ask me whether it was worth it are not satisfied with this answer. They want to know what it was like for a person who had worked for forty-five years in the private sector to work inside a large government bureaucracy. Surely it was frustrating, they prompt me. Could you get anything done?

I have to admit that it is much harder to get tangible results in the government—especially in a non-executive planning function, such as the Planning Commission's. I have to also explain that the scope of the government's responsibilities is much larger than that of any private sector company. To produce outcomes that are equitable, and not only efficient, in providing health services to all citizens, for example, is more difficult than selling medicines to only those who can pay the price that covers their cost of discovery and production. The government's job is not to make a profit. It is to improve the world for everyone. 'Making profit is easy: changing the world is hard,' was the poignant statement of a business management student at an international conference on business responsibility.

Some will persist with their interrogation of me. It is not about the difficulty of changing the world they want to know, but about changing the way the government itself functions: its red tape, its inertia, and its non-accountability to citizens. They want to know why it was so difficult to change the Planning Commission. Let me explain why.

In January 1965, I reported for duty at Bombay House, the august headquarters of the Tata group. I was sent for an induction to the group's public relations department. Faroukh Mulla, its long-time head, received me. He offered me a cup of tea that was traditionally served to directors and very senior officers in Bombay House, in fine china crockery along with cakes, by liveried waiters from the Taj Mahal Hotel in Mumbai—India's finest hotel at the time, which Tatas owned. As we sipped our tea, Mr Mulla told me about the greatness of the Tata group, as he could very well do since he was responsible for its public relations. Satisfaction began to suffuse my mind, along with the warmth of the fine tea. How lucky I was to be with the Tata group, I thought. Now I could serve the nation, and in comfort too.

As a Tata Administrative Service officer, I could be assigned to any company in the diversified Tata group: to the truck company, the chemical company, the textile company, the steel company, or even the hotels company. Faroukh Mulla asked me which one I wanted to join. The steel company, I said, having been greatly inspired by the story of its birth, as a foundation for India's industrialization that Jamsetji Tata had created in the face of opposition from the country's British rulers. When I joined the Tata Administrative Service, I had given up my intention to join the government to serve the country. I felt that to work in the steel company would be another good way to serve the country, which was my deep aspiration.

Mr Mulla noted my desire to work for Tata Steel. He then made an observation that I have never forgotten. He said, 'Maira, institutions earn their laurels. Then they begin to rest on them.' He paused, with a twinkle in his eye, and added, 'Then they "rust" on them.' I noted his clever play on words. What was the chief public relations officer of the group saying to me? I wondered. That the venerable Tata steel company was rusting on its laurels? He did not elaborate, and I dared not ask.

Resting on one's laurels was a fairly common expression. But the idea of resting leading to rusting was intriguing. Whether he was making a point about Tata Steel or even the entire Tata group, Faroukh Mulla started my learning about the interplay of success and failure in the lives of institutions, and in the lives of people too. Like the Chinese idea of Ying and Yang—each with the seed of the other in it—success can lead to failure and failure can lead to success. My explorations of the reasons why institutions succeed and why they fail went on long after I had moved on from the Tata group after twenty-five educative years, into my twenty years as a consultant to organizations and their leaders, and then into my five educative years with the Planning Commission.

Resistance to change: Five reasons

To change the way an organization functions, the behaviours of people within it and their ways of thinking must be changed. All organizations, even in the private sector, resist change. People within them are stuck in their patterns of behaviour and their habitual ways of thinking. In my fifty years of working with institutions in the private sector, the not-for-profit sector, and in the government, in leadership positions within them and as a consultant to them on bringing about change, I have learned about the nature of the 'rust' in institutions that makes them hard to change.

People resist change. We all do, even in our personal lives. How difficult it is to get one's spouse to change his or her habits. Indeed, how difficult it is to change our own habits and ways of thinking, even when we know that we must do so in our own interest! I have found that people within institutions continue to resist change until they have satisfactory answers to five questions. I will use this framework of five questions to explain why the Planning Commission was very resistant to change and to also describe the progress that was made — and indeed, progress was made.

The first question to which anyone would want an answer before they change is, 'Why change?' To stay as one is, is easy. To change into something else requires work, and can be risky too. So people stay stuck in their ways, in the rust, and they resist change. They need to be convinced that they must change in their own interest. Successful institutions get even more deeply stuck in their ways, because those ways have brought them success.

A crisis is a way to shake an institution out of the rut in which it may be rusting. A crisis, like a fire in the building or a hole in the hull of the ship, gives a compelling answer to the question, 'Why change?' We must change because we will burn or sink if we stay as we are. When a crisis becomes large and cannot be ignored any longer, people will move out of their zones of comfort and accept change. Thus, radical economic reforms became easier in India in the early 1990s when India had to ship out gold and accept assistance from the IMF. In fact, many say that further radical reforms will happen in India only when there is another national crisis. Not only countries and governments, even business corporations require crises to provide them the impetus for change. Therefore, 'the burning platform' is a metaphor that CEOs often use to make their organizations accept the need to change. We cannot stay as we are, they say, or we will die.

Crises, like a burning platform, can move people out of complacency. People realize they must move. However, crises do not provide any direction to the change after one has escaped the crisis. Once people are outside the burning theatre, or off the sinking ship or burning platform, in which direction should they proceed together?

Therefore the second question (and this is a two-part question), to which people need an answer for institutions to be transformed, is, 'What will we change to? And, would I want to go that way?' People need a vision to guide them. Moreover, as the second part of the question suggests, they must like the vision and make it their own guide for change. Otherwise, they will not change their behaviours and will continue to resist the proposed changes.

Many CEOs have tried the 'vision thing' to induce change. They share their visions widely through memos, posters, and videos. Often they are frustrated that while their visions hang around on office walls, the people in the organization, who may have initially applauded the beauty of the words, carry on as they were, their behaviours unchanged. The lesson is that it is essential that people feel the power of the vision for it to change their behaviour. Therefore, the words must be about something they deeply care about, not just what the CEO and the board care about. This explains why corporate vision statements to create more shareholder value, which had become common in the 1990s, often had hardly any effect in changing the behaviours of front-line staff and factory workers. Without changing their behaviours, shareholder value could not be increased.

Readers may recall the image of a magnet drawing arrows towards it that I described early in this book. It illustrated the point that unless a vision has the magnetic power to touch the hearts and minds of people within an organization, they will not be compelled to change. A magnetic vision that people are moved by is a 'shared vision', whereas the CEO's vision statement on the wall is merely a 'vision shared' by the CEO with limited power to affect change.

Having found a satisfactory answer to the question of what we will change to, and even liking the answer, people have another, more personal question. Which is, 'How will *I* be affected by this change?' Each person begins to compute whether he or she will be better off or worse off when the change is implemented and the vision has been realized. For example, if the corporate vision is to change from a functional organization to a customer-centric organization, people begin to wonder where they will fit into the new structure. They worry whether they will be better off or worse off. Those who fear they will have less power in the new organization will resist the change and make many arguments against it. They may add that a radical change will cause disruptions and will set the organization back and it will be better not to change it just yet. Thus, those who do not like the answer to the third question will now say they have changed their minds about the value of the vision, which was the answer to the second question and which they had liked). They even begin to deny the need for change which (the answer to the first question) they had accepted!

This was the story in the Planning Commission in 2010 and 2011. The case for change had been made by the surveys of stakeholders, all of whom had said that the Planning Commission was not making an adequate contribution to the country (with some extreme views that it was not making any contribution at all). At that time, the prime minister himself had confirmed that the Planning Commission must change. A vision of what functions the Planning Commission must perform to respond to the country's needs was outlined, which the prime minister had summarized memorably. The Planning Commission must become 'a Systems Reform Commission' and 'an essay in persuasion', rather than a budget-making body and writer of long, unread plans.

The implication of the new vision, even though not spelled out in detail, was that the Planning Commission would require very different sorts of capabilities, and much fewer people too. Apprehending this, arguments against the vision began to gather strength within the Commission. People began to justify the value of the bureaucratic routines of the Planning Commission. They said that there will be chaos in government if the Planning Commission staff did not check the proposals of the ministries and monitor the states that are ill-equipped to govern. Thus they challenged the need for any significant change in the Commission! With concern about their personal futures, they took the institutional change process back to square one, to the first question: Why change the institution?

Resistance to change for personal reasons can be overcome by assuring people that they will find a place in the new organization. However, they may still resist change. Because they have another question: 'Will I have the skills required to be effective in the new organization?' This is the fourth cause of resistance to change. For example, people may accept the need to change an organization to use technology extensively, and they may be assured that they will not be fired. However, they worry that they will not be able to function when new ways are introduced. So they propose caution while replacing time-tested processes. They even begin to extol the virtues of these old ways.

I experienced such resistance within the Planning Commission. Sam Pitroda, the chairman of the National Innovation Council, and a great advocate of electronic communication and record-keeping in the government, proposed that the cumbersome process of files, tied in proverbial red tape, moving around the government be phased out. He suggested that the Planning Commission, in whose offices he sat, should be a pioneer to bring about the change. I supported the idea. I had become very accustomed to writing my own messages and notes on my computer and retrieving discussions electronically. In fact, I was amused that every day I would be presented a big folder tied with tape, containing print-outs of the messages I had received and the replies I had already given! When I tried to explain the virtues of modern electronic communications to the Secretary of the Planning Commission, she was amused by my innocence of how the government functions. She explained the virtues of the file system. She feared that government staff would not be able to perform with new technology because they would not know how to. I heard her unspoken resistance to a change which, inside herself, she knew would be a good one.

It is wise to know the specific causes of resistance to change in an organization and to address them systematically. For example, the fear of new technology can be overcome with a systematic program of re-training. However, when the sources of resistance are not accurately understood or addressed effectively, the momentum for change will stall. Leaders who do not have skills to manage change get frustrated by the resistance to change in their organizations. They may keep reasserting the need for change. 'We must change or we will die,' they exhort again. Back to the burning platform. Back to answering the first question, whereas people in the organization, having accepted the need to change, are now seeking answers to the second, third, or fourth questions.

Examining previous unsuccessful efforts to change the Planning Commission, and applying the five-question framework, a change strategy had been worked out. Since the structural and staffing obstacles within the Planning Commission (questions three and four) were formidable, a 'Plus' would be created to provide the new capabilities the Planning Commission needed to fulfil its purpose. These capabilities would be built by leveraging resources outside the Planning Commission, anchored by a small group within it.

People have a fifth question too before they give their support to a complex transformation programme. It is, 'Does our leader have the will, and the skill, to manage this complex process?' They may have been through previous failed attempts to change the institution, in which they may have invested their emotional energy, and some may have stuck their necks out to be change-leaders. When a programme which was not well designed and well managed fails, these persons will be disheartened. Then when another change programme is launched, naturally they are cautious. They do not want to waste their energy only to get disappointed again. They decide to BOHICA (Bend Over Here It Comes Again). This too shall pass they say. Meanwhile, they give lip-service to the need for change, but carry on as they were.

Leaders need to strongly demonstrate their will and their skill to overcome the BOHICA source of resistance. They must communicate by their actions their commitment to the change. The Planning Commission had attempted to change itself a few times before and had failed to make it, as the prime minister had warned me. Therefore, its staff would be sceptical of another attempt to bring about change.

The change in the Planning Commission could not be implemented fully because its leadership did not demonstrate that it was committed to it. The deputy chairman was a reluctant reformer. The disconnection of the top leadership from the transformation of the Planning Commission became painfully evident in the last meeting of the Planning Commission on 30 April 2014. The prime minister, the chairman of the Commission, came to say a thank you and a farewell. He concluded the meeting by asking four questions about the Planning Commission:

1. Are we using tools and approaches which were designed for a different era?
2. Have we added on new functions and layers without any restructuring of the more traditional activities in the Commission?
3. What additional roles should the Planning Commission play and what capacities does it need to ensure it continues to be relevant to the growth process?
4. Governance issues being integral to economic growth, are these areas of the Planning Commission to delve into?

I was completely taken aback. Had he not asked similar questions in 2009 about the Planning Commission's relevance in the new millennium? Had we not given him the answers to these questions in 2010, which he had approved of? Had we not been struggling to implement the changes required, which he was aware of? So why was he asking these questions again? And what did he expect should be done by the Planning Commission he was addressing which would be resigning, along with him, within a month since a new government had been elected already?

So, were my five years of effort to change the way in which the Planning Commission functioned worth it, if the prime minister, its head, seemed oblivious of them finally?

The first big institutional reform that the new prime minister, Mr Narendra Modi announced was from the ramparts of the Red Fort on 15 August 2014. It was the disbanding of the Planning Commission to make way for a new institution to serve modern India's needs. The new institution, the NITI Aayog, was announced on 1 January 2015. The charter of this institution is well in line with the directions for change of the Planning Commission that had been developed (but which Prime Minister Dr Manmohan Singh, strangely did not recall in his farewell speech on 30 April 2014).

'Why change?' and 'What shall we change to?' are the first two sources of resistance to change. When a vehicle is stuck deeply in a rut, often people are required just to push it out and put it onto the road. Thereafter, the driver of the vehicle must take over and carry on the journey of change. Those who helped to push it out of the rut can then step back and wipe their brows, with some satisfaction that they too had a role in enabling progress to be made.

I do get satisfaction that the planning institution was finally shaken out of the rut in which it was stuck and the rust in which it was entrapped, and that it has been directed onto a new course. Now the driver in the seat must step on the gas and steer it.

SEVEN

COOPERATION SYSTEMS

It is difficult to change an organization. Transforming a country is much harder. The new organization that has replaced the Planning Commission is called the National Institution for Transforming India (NITI Aayog). It is expected to do more transforming and less planning.

Transforming a company to produce more value for its shareholders is easy compared with transforming a vast country to produce value for its very diverse citizens, especially a democratic country like India.

I wrote my first book on organizational transformation, *The Accelerating Organization: Embracing the Face of Human Change,** in 1996. Then I was living in the Boston area in the US and was consulting to many corporations in the US, Europe, and South America. There I met an Indian civil servant, who was attending a programme at the Kennedy School of Government at the Harvard University, who had read my book and liked it. He compared my ideas with what he was learning in the programme at the Kennedy School. He pointed out that there was a difference in kind, not merely in scale, between the work of government leaders and corporate leaders. He suggested I read a book by one of the teachers at the Kennedy School,

---

*Peter B. Scott-Morgan, and Arun Maira. *The Accelerating Organization: Embracing the Face of Human Change.* McGraw-Hill, 1997.

Mark Moore, which I immediately did. In his book, *Creating Public Value: Strategic Management in Government,** Moore describes the difficulty in determining what the 'public' will value and obtaining an agreement about that, in comparison with defining what 'customers' will value and then efficiently delivering that. Consider the public goods that citizens expect governments to deliver, such as security, public health, and an equitable system of education. In some cases, the public good is a 'product', such as 24X7 clean water. But in many cases the public good that must be produced is intangible: such as equity, fairness, and access to opportunities.

Corporations need to invest financial resources to make products and deliver them to customers and thus provide value to customers. Corporations raise the funds they need from investors. For this, in addition to the requirements of their customers, corporate leaders must understand what their investors value and deliver it to them. Therefore, corporate leaders strive to increase the shareholder value of their corporations. Shareholder value can be measured in financial numbers, which are easier to compute than intangible measures of public value.

Moreover, resources required for producing public goods of which only some citizens may be the beneficiaries must come from those who have the resources, from taxes on these people. What do these investors in the public good get in return? Their returns cannot be explained in simple terms, as they can to investors in private enterprises. Though difficult to make, the case has to be made, and there must be an implicit contract that is made as explicit as it can be, with benefits that are neither financial nor even quantifiable, that can nevertheless be appreciated by 'investors' in public goods.

---

*Mark Moore. *Creating Public Value: Strategic Management in Government.* Harvard University Press, Reprint in 1997.

Thus, a critical difference between processes of making public policy and corporate strategy is in the 'up-front' activity of engaging with citizens to clarify the purpose of the policy. Mark Moore says: 'We might think of this activity as helping to define rather than create public value. But this activity also creates value since it satisfies the desire of citizens for a well-ordered society in which fair, efficient, and accountable public enterprises exist.' In other words, the quality of the process of making public policy is in itself a public good of great value that a government must create for its citizens.

There are three reasons to emphasize the need for good 'process' in public policy. The first is that good process is necessary to produce the specific deliverables of a policy. The second is that good processes for making public policy increases citizens' trust in the institutions that govern their lives. The third is that multi-stakeholder processes increase social solidarity.

Participative processes

Public policy is a process by which a government and citizens co-create public value. The concept of co-creating value is entering into the corporate world too. Valued products must be produced for customers by corporate managers, but products that customers will value must be conceived with customers too.

Listening to citizens is not as simple as listening to customers. Economist A.O. Hirschman explains the difference in his book, *Exit, Voice, and Loyalty*.* He points out that the way customers signal their displeasure to corporations is by not buying the firm's products—in other words by 'exiting'.

---

*A.O. Hirschman. *Exit, Voice and Loyalty: Responses to Decline in Firms.* Harvard University Press, 1970.

Their voice is clearly expressed — yea or nay — by their decision to purchase or not. On the other hand, citizens do not exit the country. Indeed, they cannot, because they cannot leave and they cannot be banished. If they are displeased, they may speak up. However, when they speak, what they are saying is not always clear.

Hirschman points out that Milton Friedman, who famously decreed that the business of business must only be business, had expressed his difficulty in accepting the notion that people should desire to express their views to make them prevail. Friedman describes the people's desire to be heard as a resort to 'cumbrous political channels'. He would much rather they resort to 'efficient market mechanisms' and use their money rather than their mouths to make their opinions known.

In the market we are customers, and can speak with the precise language of money — if we have it. In society we are citizens, and speak with our minds and hearts, in many languages and many forms of expression.

Processes for participative planning and democratic deliberation are essential for the transformation of a democratic country such as India. Deliberation and planning when people have different perspectives, different values, and different ideologies is cumbersome, but it must be done. Simple processes to perform these functions effectively must be found, developed, disseminated, and applied. This is the task the India Backbone Implementation Network was created to perform. This is the task that the National Institution for Transforming India (NITI Aayog) has been set up to do.

Leadership by persuasion

Another critical difference between organizations and countries (especially democratic countries) is in the source of the leaders' authorities. Within an organization, the leader has structural authority over others. He can hire and fire them, albeit with due process. The leader is appointed from above, and not by the people below. The CEO of a corporation is appointed by the board above and is accountable to it, whereas a leader in a democratic government is appointed by the people below, who can fire him (or her) at election time.

A further complication for leaders in government is that they require the cooperation of many stakeholders to produce public value, as explained before, with more complex processes for obtaining their cooperation. They have to form cooperation systems to produce results, and cannot demand cooperation by exercising structural authority that they do not have, over those whose efforts have to be directed to produce the outcomes desired.

Ronald Reagan once said, 'Government is not the solution: it is the problem.' Corporate leaders adopted this slogan. In the heady days of corporate capitalism and the Washington Consensus, from the early 1990s till the global financial crisis in 2008 when the value of government and regulation of corporations began to be realized again, corporate CEOs were celebrated as the models to follow. Even heads of government began to refer to themselves as CEOs.

The differences between the responsibilities of corporate CEOs and government leaders were glossed over and limitations of the 'CEO model' for government were ignored. In those days, Jack Welch was amongst the most celebrated CEOs in the world. He had created enormous value for GE's shareholders. He had a reputation for toughness: for insisting that every year the poorest performers must be removed from GE, and for down-sizing the workforce whenever hard times came. He acquired companies and sold them to increase GE's shareholder value. His methods became 'best practices' that were taught in business schools and were propagated by management consultants.

Imagine the head of a country, even an unelected one. When times are tough, can he ship out people from the country to reduce the burden on national finances? Can he buy and sell other countries to increase his country's GDP when economists express concern with its decline? The instruments that leaders of governments and leaders in the corporate world can use to produce results for their stakeholders are different and must be so.

In cooperation systems, the power to induce collaboration, and the power to ensure coordination, does not come from an authority above. It must come from within the system. The power lies within, and amongst the partners. 'Cooperation systems' work with strong lateral processes, whereas traditional 'organizations', in the corporate sector and in government too, rely on vertical processes of authority for coordination.

Within an organization, leaders can use the powers of their positions in the hierarchy, and the authority they have over others, and demand compliance and get things done. When cooperation of others is required who are outside the boundaries of the organization, other methods must be used to enrol them voluntarily in a larger enterprise, and evoke their commitment for a larger cause.

Project management techniques can convert confusion into coordination. They cannot convert contention into collaboration. For that, other disciplines are required, of stakeholder engagement, dialogue, and participative governance of programmes. Several chief ministers of Indian states are establishing 'Programme Management Offices' to expedite implementation of programmes and projects. Data about who has to do what by when is loaded onto a central system, and progress is monitored. Those who fail to perform on time are pulled up. Thus, projects can be expedited.

When the resistance arises from affected stakeholders

who are not within the organization, who do not accept the goals of the programme, or fear that the ways in which the goals are planned to be achieved will harm them, a 'CEO-like' authority cannot be used to make them comply. In these situations, and there are many of these in a democracy going through a process of economic development and change, the 'upstream' engagement of stakeholders to convert potential (or manifest) contentions into collaboration must precede the 'downstream' process of project management for converting confusion in execution into coordination.

The NITI Aayog (the National Institution for Transforming India) must promote cooperative federalism because the central government cannot impose its authority on the states to produce results. The NITI Aayog must promote planning in villages and towns, by the people, for the people, and not by government functionaries ordering the people around. 'Minimum government; maximum governance', which the prime minister says must be promoted, requires officers in government right down the line, from central government ministries to district level officials, to learn new skills for leading by persuasion and not with positional authority. The NITI Aayog will itself have to learn these new ways to be an 'essay in persuasion' and a 'Systems Reform Commission'.

Even if officers in the government have acknowledged the need for change in the country, and even if they intellectually accept the vision of democratic and devolved processes of governance which the prime minister is extolling, they will find it difficult to function in new ways. They will be unhappy with the reduction in their importance. And they will not have the skills required to operate in new ways. Therefore, while government officers will not oppose the need for change, or intellectually oppose the vision, they will resist it. They are uncomfortable because they are not getting satisfactory answers to the third and the fourth questions in the five-question framework for diagnosing and treating sources of change resistance during transformation processes, explained in the previous chapter.

Such resistance can be overcome if the officers are provided with the tools and skills with which they can be effective. I have found that most officers in the government have great motivation to serve the country. They are also proud that India is a democracy. They need to learn twenty-first-century methods of leadership in cooperation systems. The India Backbone Implementation Network (IbIn), the start-up idea incubated by the Planning Commission, began a process of finding, disseminating, and applying such methods. Some principles of these methods have been illustrated in the three projects reported in the previous chapters.

The IbIn Knowledge Compendium, with the principles and methods, has been handed over to the NITI Aayog and the PMO. They will have to decide how they will bring the vision of a democratic, diverse, and developed India to life.

In the interval of nine months from the close of the Planning Commission until the NITI Aayog got going, the IbIn idea was kept alive and expanded by the start-up team operating from their 'dug-out' in the India@75 premises in Gurgaon. The dug-out is now empty. All the members of the start-up have proceeded on their several journeys of change and learning.

ENDS AND BEGINNINGS

'The moving finger writes, and having writ moves on..' wrote the poet, Omar Khayyam. Journeys end, and the journey goes on. The book has come to an end, but its stories continue.

I began the book with the admission that as a young boy, I wanted to serve the country and the people in the only way I knew how to then, which was to join the government. I could not, and I decided to retire gracefully when I was sixty-five, and learn to play golf. Then, while riding in a tram in Prague in June 2009, I accepted Prime Minister Manmohan Singh's unexpected phone call to join the Planning Commission and serve the country.

That period of service that began with that phone call on a tram in Prague came to end in June 2014 when, as is customary, I resigned from the Planning Commission when the a new government was elected. The Planning Commission was laid to rest by the new prime minister, Narendra Modi, on 15 August 2014. Nevertheless, the spirit of IbIn (Abhi India and Abhi In) moved along—'It is India's time now', and 'all must be in'.

Out of the blue, in November 2014, I received a request from some young Indians to help them with something unusual. They called themselves GAP—Global Action against Poverty. They had an idea for an unusual meeting in the

Sabarmati Ashram on 12 March 2015. It was the anniversary of the day Mahatma Gandhi had begun the long Dandi March from the ashram to raise salt from the sea. Millions joined him as he marched on to claim from their foreign rulers the people's rights to their land and their own salt.

The GAP team had invited Professor Mohammed Yunus, the founder of the Grameen Bank and winner of the Nobel Peace Prize, Elabhen Bhat, founder of the remarkable SEWA organization in India, Bill Drayton, founder of the Asoka Foundation, and seven other remarkable persons to the meeting at Sabarmati. The GAP team were proposing to invite 200 others who, like themselves, were already making some efforts to reduce poverty in their surroundings. These change-makers wanted to have more impact but did not know how.

The GAP team asked me to curate the meeting and extract the recipe of the 'secret sauce' these remarkable persons knew and pass it on to the 200 change-makers looking for it. Their aim was to produce 200 better empowered and wiser change-makers who would leave the ashram with clear action plans about how they would go about changing the world.

Changing the world is not an engineering exercise, I told them. It cannot be reduced to a series of pre-determined mechanical steps. There is an inner journey, within the change-maker, that must be undertaken too. Persons who change the world are like fireflies with an inner light. They are life-long learners, I suggested. Consider the title of Mahatma Gandhi's own story, his autobiography—*My Experiments with Truth.*

The change-makers must be prepared to extract the secret sauce not only from the great leaders they would meet in the ashram but from within themselves too. They should introspect: what drives them to change the world, and what would they need to learn to have more impact on it? I said their journey plans would be along three tracks: a track of actions, a track of creating new partnerships, and a track of learning.

I asked the GAP team to prepare themselves for the meeting. I requested them to think about their own journeys and their own plans and, as their first steps to learn, to share their stories with each other and with me.

One of them asked me, what about my plan? What did I want to do, now that I was out of the hurly-burly of working within the government? What did I want to learn? Would I learn to play golf now that I would have time for it? He made me think.

Here is the plan I submitted to the GAP team.

MY PLAN

My favourite carol is the 'Little Drummer Boy'. He says he has no wealth to offer the Lord Jesus. All he has is his drum, which he will play for the baby Jesus. His offering is the 'rump-a-rum-pump' of his drum, which he will play at his very best for the Lord.

I began to read the Bhagavad Gita when I was a teenager, almost sixty years ago. I have been fixed since then on lines in the second chapter, to which I return again and again. 'You only have a right to the work, and not to the fruits thereof.' The Gita preaches detachment from the fruits. What are the fruits of the work? The obvious interpretation of the fruits are the benefits for oneself. What about the achievement of the goal? Is it not a fruit of the work? Should not one seek the goal or should one strive only to do good work and do it well? Is this the meaning of the 'right to the work', which is all that one must have?

I read the philosopher Eric Fromm's classic book, *To Have or to Be?* when I was in my thirties. He contrasts two ways of living and achieving. One is a striving to have more. The other is a journey to become a better being. I was then in the midst of a challenging project to ensure that my company—an under-resourced Indian company that had ventured into foreign waters—could beat the biggest and the best of the world in a foreign market in which the others were already entrenched. I was the designated leader. We did beat them and achieve our goal. Fromm stirred many questions in me. What was my role in this achievement? Did I deserve credit for it?

As I have grown older, which is inevitable, I have been drawn to the ancient Indian wisdom of adjusting one's work to the stage of one's life. There is a long stage, in the middle of one's life, when one must play the role of the 'householder' and play it well. At that stage one is the producer, of children, of wealth to support them, and of achievements (while following the Gita's dictum of the right to the work and not the fruits). That stage must pass, and another must come when one must give up those pursuits, to reflect on who one is, and concentrate on becoming a better being.

I have asked myself many times in my life, when I have paused to reflect, what is the work that I aspire to do well? The answer has come, softly first and louder now, that I want to help others to work with others so that they can produce the results they want.

I want to play the drum. Provide the rhythm in the background that enables others to coordinate their music. And I want to play it well.

The percussionist—the drummer or tabla player—is not the player of the melody, or the singer of the song. When many instruments are playing and many voices are singing, the percussion enables them to play and sing in unison.

I have sung songs and sung them well, too, when I was in that phase of my life when it was my role to be the singer. I have done my fifty years. Now others must sing and play, and I would like to provide them the rhythm, if they want it, to help them perform better while they are on the stage.

My aspiration now is to be a better drummer, and a better being.

My action plan is to assist people who want a drummer. How should a drummer measure his success? By the large numbers of concerts he has played in? Or the quality of the concerts even if they were very few? At this stage in my life, when time will become scarcer, as it inevitably must, it is quality, not quantity that I aspire for.

My collaboration plan is to be selective about who I engage with. I must be selective because time is scarce, and there is none to waste. I must engage with those who really want a drummer: not because it is customary to have one but because they know that without a drummer they cannot achieve what they want to.

My learning plan is to learn to restrain myself from wasting my time on what is popular, and what gives passing fame. To learn to say 'No' to the greed to have more popularity, more approbation, more followers.

A story from Chris Bonnington's compilation of stories of great adventurers and sportsmen that I read thirty-five years ago,* when I was struggling with the lines from the second chapter of the Gita (which I still am) continues to haunt me. It is an account of a round-the-world solo yacht race.

The winner, way ahead of the others, had rounded the tip of South America from the Pacific to the Atlantic Ocean. As he was sailing up towards London, towards the finish, he heard on his radio of the preparations for his reception. The Queen would come, and the media of course, in droves. He thought about it. Was this why he was racing—the fruits of success? Or was it for good sailing at his best? He turned his boat around, to sail down the Atlantic and around the Cape of Good Hope into the Indian Ocean, to complete another solo circumnavigation of the earth!

I must be better. I must learn the dynamics within ensembles of players and singers—what makes it difficult for them to coordinate and what would enable them to play better together to produce music that will uplift the world. My learning plan is to learn to play the drum better.

---

*Chris Bonnington. *Quest for Adventure*. Random House, 1983.

I end with lines from Robert Frost's 'Two Tramps at Mud-Time':

> But yield who will to their separation,
> My object in living is to unite
> My avocation and my vocation
> As my two eyes make one in sight.
> Only where love and need are one,
> And the work is play for mortal stakes,
> Is the deed ever really done
> For Heaven and the future's sakes.

ACKNOWLEDGEMENTS

This is a book about my experiences. And about ideas shaped by those experiences. Several ideas have been stimulated by thought-leaders who I encountered as I was living through my experiences. They gave me lenses through which I could make sense of my own experiences. I got to know some of these thought-leaders personally, by working with them, and many only through their books. I have named many of these people in this book: who gave me the opportunities to have the experiences I had and to learn from them; and thought-leaders who gave me ideas that shaped my ways of seeing the world.

When I finished writing the book, read and re-read it, and sat back to acknowledge all those who have helped me assemble content for this book, by the stimuli of opportunities to experience, and by the ideas they have given me, the names kept bubbling up unstoppably. This is a book of many journeys of change and learning over many decades, several interwoven with each other too. I find it impossible to name the myriad people I owe so much too. I thank all these teachers, many of whom never even knew I existed. This book could be because you have enabled it.

The book is because some other people made the book happen. They helped me with the writing of it. First, my wife, Shama. 'Don't rush it,' she would caution me. 'Don't worry about dead-lines; write a good book.' When I had my manuscript ready, (and my publisher was pleased with my timeliness), she was not satisfied I had done my best yet. So I decided to ask a writer whose quality of writing I admire, to check it out for me.

Charles Assisi, who was very busy with a new venture he was starting, nevertheless very kindly agreed to do me a favour and read the manuscript. He called me a few days later and said that he had to be brutal. He did not like the way I had written the book. He could not hear the voice of the writer. So I wrote the book all over again! Then he read the new version but I sensed he was not completely satisfied. So I changed it again. My wife was delighted to see me work at it again and again.

Ritu Vajpeyi-Mohan, my publisher at Rupa, was also happy that I was being put to work by Charles and my wife to produce a better book. I thank her for giving me the opportunity to have this book published; and thank her, Amrita Mukherji, Sayantan Ghosh and the staff at Rupa, for their patience and support during its production.

Finally I thank my grandson, Viren, who had written a book on India's Planning Commission before I wrote this book—when he was seven years old. I have reproduced some pages from his book in mine. I showed him the final manuscript, after all the changes were made. I asked him for permission to quote his work. For the record, he was very amused and graciously agreed.

Index

The Accelerating Organization: Embracing the Face of Human Change, 69, 227
Ahluwalia, Montek Singh, 4, 7–8, 13, 88, 90, 92, 104, 115, 129, 141, 171, 183
Alexander the Great, 47–48
Ambani, Mukesh, 179
Anderson, Phil, 130
anti-corruption movements, 140
application, 28
'appreciating assets' of an enterprise, 193–196
Approach Paper, 101, 108–109
Arab-Malaysian Bank, 44
Arrow, Kenneth, 130
Arthur, Brian, 130
Arthur D. Little Inc. (ADL), 63
aspiration, 67–69
Automobile Component Manufacturers Association (ACMA), 192

Bain and Company study on human resources, 193–194, 198
Bendahara, Tengku Arif, 42
Bhalla, Shipra, 174
Bharat Gears, 191
Bhat, Elaben, 236
Birla, Anjali, 174

Birla, Kumar Mangalam, 179
BOHICA (Bend Over Here It Comes Again), 224
Bonnington, Chris, 240
business regulatory environment
  challenges for improving, 185–186
  impact of, 177–180

capacity-building process, 212
Caterpillar, 62
Centre for Study of Science, Technology and Policy (CSTEP), 131
change process in public sector, 210–211
Chibber, Vivek
  Locked in Place: State-Building and Late Industrialization, 82
China, 147–148
  GDP, 148
  manufacturing sector, 152–153
  side-effects of focusing on special coastal zones, 150–151
  trajectories of development, 161–162
Chinese business people, 52
Choksi, Rustum, 29

CII, 123
CII (the Confederation of Indian Industry), 116, 123, 172, 179, 190
civil services examination, 24–26, 29
collaborative planning and implementation, 164, 174
Communist parties, 8
community-based and collaborative governance, 133, 163
computer-numerically-controlled (CNC) machines, 60
consulting organizations, 14–15
contract employment, 198–199
convergent planning, 208–211
cooperation systems, 231–234
cooperative federalism, 214, 233
cotton industry, 30

Daimler-Benz, 32–33
Das, Tarun, 116
Deming, Prof., 165, 193
development
    collaborative planning and implementation, 164, 167–168, 174
    comparison of China's and India's trajectories, 161–162
    strategies to reach India's aspirational scenario, 163
    Total Quality Management (TQM) approach, 164–167
Doing Business methodology, 181
Drayton, Bill, 236
dual citizenship, 6–7
Dubey, Rajeev, 196

economic reforms of 1990s, 9, 92, 149
e-governance projects, 86
entrepreneurial start-up within government, 17–19, 27

Fauconnier, Henri, 46
Francis, Ajith, 8, 175
Friedman, Milton, 82, 230
Fromm, Eric
    To Have or To Be?, 238
Frost, Robert, 31
    'Two Tramps at Mud-Time', 241
fundamental rights, 152

Gandhi, Mahatma, 8, 30, 152, 209, 236
Gandhi, Rajiv, 4, 115
GDP growth of India, 122, 128, 132, 144, 188
    comparison with China, 147–148
    in different plausible scenarios, 134–136
    Goldman Sachs' projection, 147
    trajectories of development, 161–162
Gell-Mann, Murray, 130
General Motors, 58, 65
Germany, 81, 154
GIZ (Deutsche Gesellschaft fur Internationale Zusammenarbeit), 167–168
Global Action against Poverty (GAP), 235–237
    suggested action, collaboration, and learning plan, 238–241

Goldratt, Eli, 157
Gopalakrishnan, R., 13
Gupta, Kavita, 196

Hameed, Syeda, 105
Hindustan Machine Tools (HMT), 60
Hino, 54
Hirschman, A.O.
  Exit, Voice, and Loyalty, 229
Honda Motor Company, 66
hydroelectric power plants, 30

ICICI Bank, 18, 174
implementation problem in India, 155–156, 161, 184–185
India, World Bank's low rating of, 187
India Backbone Implementation Network (IbIn), 27, 158, 169–175, 201
  collaborative planning and implementation, 174–175
  concept, 168
  dialogue process between unions and employers, 201–204
  Knowledge Compendium, 168, 234
  methods of collaborative scenario planning, 173
  simple systems of effective participative planning, 212–213
Indian economy, modeling, 129–131
Indian Institute of Fundamental Research, Mumbai, 30
Indian Institute of Science, Bangalore, 30

India's manufacturing sector, post-liberalization era, 9
IndiaWorks High Five, 168
industrialization, 194
industrial licensing, 56
industrial relations, 190–191
  dialogue between the unions and employers, 201–204
  and labour practices, 197–198
  need for trust, 203
Innovation Associates, 64
institution
  modifying, 86
  sketch of an, 85–86
Ishikawa, Prof., 165

Jaikumar, Prof., 157
Jaipur Leadership Conclave, 123–124
Jakatdar, Sharad, 36–37
Japanese approach to quality, 165–167
Japanese companies in India, 56
Japanese light trucks and cars, 63
Jayalalithaa, Ms., 103
job creation in India, 148–149, 153–158
Juran, Joseph M., 193

Kahane, Adam, 112, 117–119, 173–174
Kapur, Surinder, 17, 190–191, 196
Kennedy, John F., 58
Khan, General Jehangir, 21
Khan, Nusrat Fateh Ali, 21
Kieffer, Charlie, 64

Kipling, Rudyard, 22–23
'knowledge management'
    system, 187
Krishnamurthy, V., 150, 151

labour laws, 182, 198
    dialogue to reform, 198–203
labour 'markets' in India,
    193–196
Laxman, R.K.
    *Remaking India: One Country,
    One Destiny*, 110
Leadership Conclaves, 123
learning cycle, 187–189
Lehman Brothers collapse, 128
L&T, 18

Mahajan, Bhavana, 18
Mahindra, Anand, 14
Mahindra group, 14
'Make in India' strategy, 178
Manuel, Trevor, 180
manufacturing policy of India,
    150
    bottlenecks, 158
    collaboration and
        coordination, need for
        improving, 183–187
    conceptual and ideological
        problems, 182–183
    good industrial relations
        practices, 182–183
    and issues of Micro, Small,
        and Medium Enterprises
        (MSME), 178–180
    promotion of small and
        medium industries, 151
    strategies to grow
        manufacturing sector,
        153–158

tax regimes and labour laws,
    182
Mazda, 56
Meena, Manish, 174
Mehrotra, Shruti, 17
memories
    house in Lahore, 20–21
    independence and partition,
        21–22
    mother's lessons in living,
        28–29
    private sector employment,
        25
    schooling and college
        education, 22–25
    Tata selection test, 29–31
Micro, Small, and Medium
    Enterprises (MSME), issues
    of, 178–180
    regional issues, 180–181
Minimalist Manufacturing, 157
Mitsubishi, 43, 56
Modi, Narendra, 103–104, 143,
    178, 225, 235
Moily, Veerappa, 183
Moolgaokar, Sumant, 34–38,
    60
    on human capital, 39
Moore, Mark, 228–229
    *Creating Public Value: Strategic
    Management in Government*,
    228
Mulla, Faroukh, 217

Naipaul, V.S.
    India: A Million Mutinies Now,
    157
    India: An Area of Darkness, 38
    India: A Wounded Civilization,
    38, 158

NASA, 63–64

Nath, Arjun, 16–18, 155

National Council of Applied Economic Research (NCAER), 127, 134, 136–137

National Development Council, 101

National Investment and Manufacturing Zones, India, 152

National Manufacturing Competitiveness Council, 150–151

Nehru, Jawaharlal, 32

Niebuhr, Reinhold, 14, 112

network-based models of enterprises, 134

Nissan, 43, 56

NITI Aayog (National Institution for Transforming India), 143–144, 189, 213, 226, 227, 233–234

Nohwar, Arjun, 17, 174

Ogra, Surbhi, 174

OIC (Overseas Indian Citizen) card, 7

Oxford Forecasting Group, 127

Palkhivala, Nani, 41

Pan, Lim Tek, 52

Paradigm Consulting, 15–19, 155, 166, 171, 174

Patwa, Abhinav, 174

Pemandu–Sakal methodology, 206–211, 213

Peng, Deng Xiao, 153

performance management of ministries, 95–96

phased manufacturing program, 57

Pillai, Sudha, 141

PIO (Person of Indian Origin) card, 7

Pitroda, Sam, 65, 223

Planning Commission, 32

Planning Commission, service at, 3–9, 235. *see also* scenario planning process; *scenarios of India's future*

approvals to recruit outside the commission, 13–18

'Big Fight', 8

facilities and staff, 10–11

issue of citizenship, 6–7, 215

leadership development opportunity, 17–18

Left parties opposition, 8

setting of new paradigm of organization, 13–19

Planning Commission of India, 79–84, 216

Government Resolution of 1950, 83, 101

organization in Tagore's *Gitanjali*, 95

planning process of 12th Five Year Plan. *see* planning process of 12th Five Year Plan

preparing Five Year Plans, 94–95

processes within, 87–88

resistance to change, 218, 222–226

strategies for change, 88–93

as 'Systems Reform' Commission, 111

Viren's perception, 76–78
planning process of 12th Five
Year Plan, 94–100, 139–140.
see also scenario planning
process
*Approaching Equity: Civil
Society Inputs for the
Approach Paper-12th Five
Year Plan*, 105–106
chief ministers' reaction,
102–105
civil society organizations
(CSOs) participation,
105–107
draft of the Approach Paper,
108–109, 114–115
jobs and livelihoods, 144–146
National Development
Council, role of, 101
process to inputs from
stakeholders, 102
reform of governance and
planning institutions,
142–144
Wada Na Todo Abhiyan
(WTNA), 105–106, 131
Posco, 156
Prabhu-Coelho, Siddharth, 18
private sector employment, 25
process re-engineering projects,
86
'Programme Management
Offices,' 232
Project Jupiter, 59, 67
breakthrough performance of,
65
challenges, 57–58
development process, 59
'encircle' strategy, 62
introduction of innovative

HR practice and CNC
machines, 60–61
Project Saturn, 58
public policy, developing,
228–229
'CEO model' for government,
231
critical difference between
corporate strategy and, 229
methods of leadership,
230–234
need for participative
processes, 229–230
public sector, change process
in, 210–211
Pune Bus Day, 205–206
Pemandu-Sakal methodology
for implementing, 206–211
Pusa Agriculture Institute,
98–99
Putte, Alexander van de, 125

Radhakrishnan, S., 24
Raghavan, Varoon, 15–17, 155
Rai, Deepak, 53
rainbow nation, 113
Raje, Vasundhara, 124, 212
Ramchandran, Sriram, 15–17,
155, 157
Rampur Engineering Company,
22
Rangan, Kasturi, 129
Rao, Narasimha, 115
Reagan, Ronald, 231
*Remaking India: One Country,
One Destiny*, 69
resistance to change, 218–222,
233
RFD (Results Framework
Document) process, 95–96

Sakal Group
  capacity-building process, 211
  Delivering Change
    Foundation (DCF), 213
  Pune Bus Day, implementing,
    205–211
Sakal Marathi, 205–206
Samant, Datta, 191
Sardesai, Rajdeep, 8
Saxena, N.C., 90, 92
scenario planning process,
  111–113
  for BRICs countries, 122–123
  brief history, 116
  case of Shell Oil company,
    116–117
  in context of India, 117–121,
    125–137
  Leadership Conclaves,
    123–125
  Mont Fleur scenario
    planning, 116
  people perception about
    India, 120
scenarios of India's future,
  137–138, 142
  Atakta Bharat ('India
    stalling'), 126–128, 162
  BollyWorld, 126–128
  'Falling Apart' scenario,
    135–136
  findings, 132–134
  'Muddling Along' scenario,
    136
  'Pahale India' ('India first'),
    127–128
  'The Flotilla Advances'
    scenario, 134–135
Sen, Pronab, 97, 100
Senge, Peter, 64

Seth, Anand, 17
Shama, 4–5, 7
*Shaping the Future: Aspirational
  Leadership in India and
  Beyond*, 69
shared aspirational vision,
  70–71
shareholder value, 228
Sharma, Anand, 150
Sharma, Shikha, 17
Shrivastava, Harsh, 99–100
Singh, Manmohan, 4, 7, 79,
  84–85, 92, 100, 101, 115,
  150, 226, 235
Sinha, Alok, 174–175
skill development, 182, 196
Sona Steering, 191
The Soul of Malaya, 46
South Africa, scenario planning
  process of, 112–113
Soviet model of planning, 80,
  82, 116
St Stephen's College, 4, 24, 26
strategies for change, 88–93
  creating a 'Plus,' 93
  decision-criteria, 89
  institutional change
    programs, 93
  structural reform, 90
Sustainable Economic
  Development Assessment
  (SEDA) framework, 144

Tanishka movement, 207, 209
Tata, Jamsetji, 29–30, 217
Tata, Ratan, 80, 179
Tata Administrative Services
  (TAS), 4, 8, 13–14, 215,
  217–218
  manpower plans, 36

in strategic planning, 32
Tatab assignment, 46, 67
   aim of, 48
   analysis of Tatab
      management, 48–51
   dealing with Chinese
      business people, 52–53
   getting spare parts, 53–54
   innovations in management
      of sales, service,
      distribution, and
      production, 51–52
   Japanese appreciation, 54–55
   round-the-clock service
      centres, 53
Tata Engineering and
   Locomotive Company, 32
Tata Group, 29–30, 215, 217
   mission of, 32
   move from Make in India to
      Made by India, 33–35
   Tata-Daimler joint venture,
      32–34
Tata Iron and Steel Company,
   30
Tata Steel, 218
TELCO, Pune, 32, 34–40,
   156
   CNC machines, 60
   innovative HR practice, 60–61
   manufacturing of light
      commercial vehicles, 57–66
   Moolgaokar's vision as 'a
      learning factory,' 39
   paying for skills vs paying
      for output, 40
   Tatab joint-venture issue,
      39–45. see also Tatab
      assignment

theories-in-use for governance,
   133–134, 137, 171
'Three Whys' process, 155
Tiwari, Pragya, 174
Total Quality Management
   (TQM), 164–167, 170, 192
Toyota, 56
Toyota Motor Company, 165
Toyota Production System, 64
   transforming a company, 227
Trivedi, Prajapati, 95

Ultra-Mega Power Plants
   (UMPPs), 156
United Progressive Alliance
   (UPA), 3

Vajpayee, Atal Bihari, 99, 188
Viren, 12, 75–76
   perception of Planning
      Commission (or
      Community), 76–78
Vittal, N., 119

Wada Na Todo Abhiyan
   (WTNA), 105–106, 131
Waldorp, M. Mitchel
   Complexity: The Emerging Science
      at the Edge of Order and
      Chaos, 130
'Water for All' program, 210, 212
Welch, Jack, 231
World Bank, 167–168
   Doing Business report, 180–182
   low rating of India, 187
World Economic Forum (WEF),
   122–125

Yunus, Prof. Mohammed, 236

www.ingramcontent.com/pod-product-compliance
Lightning Source LLC
Chambersburg PA
CBHW050231270326
41914CB00033BA/1872/J